Masonic Symbolism Of The Bible

Chalmers I. Paton

Kessinger Publishing's Rare Reprints

Thousands of Scarce and Hard-to-Find Books on These and other Subjects!

- Americana
- Ancient Mysteries
- Animals
- Anthropology
- Architecture
- Arts
- Astrology
- Bibliographies
- Biographies & Memoirs
- Body, Mind & Spirit
- Business & Investing
- Children & Young Adult
- Collectibles
- Comparative Religions
- Crafts & Hobbies
- Earth Sciences
- Education
- Ephemera
- Fiction
- Folklore
- Geography
- Health & Diet
- History
- Hobbies & Leisure
- Humor
- Illustrated Books
- Language & Culture
- Law
- Life Sciences
- Literature
- Medicine & Pharmacy
- Metaphysical
- Music
- Mystery & Crime
- Mythology
- Natural History
- Outdoor & Nature
- Philosophy
- Poetry
- Political Science
- Science
- Psychiatry & Psychology
- Reference
- Religion & Spiritualism
- Rhetoric
- Sacred Books
- Science Fiction
- Science & Technology
- Self-Help
- Social Sciences
- Symbolism
- Theatre & Drama
- Theology
- Travel & Explorations
- War & Military
- Women
- Yoga
- *Plus Much More!*

We kindly invite you to view our catalog list at:
http://www.kessinger.net

CHAPTER LXII.

Masonic Symbols.—The Bible.

THE Word of God is the great light of Masonry, and therefore a Bible forms a necessary part of the *furniture* of every Lodge, and is placed open upon the Altar, and along with it the Square and Compasses. An open Bible is carried in all masonic processions, by an office-bearer styled the Bible-bearer. The Bible is also variously used as a masonic symbol, the square and compasses being generally depicted along with it, for reasons to be hereafter mentioned. At present, however, let us confine our attention to the Bible itself.

Freemasonry recognises the Light of Nature; but it acknowledges the insufficiency of that light for the illumination of the darkness of the world and the guidance of man in the path of duty and of safety. With great gratitude do we receive that light of revelation which it has pleased God to impart; and the prominent—it may be said, the primary—place which is assigned to the Bible in masonic symbolism, is not merely on account of the divine law contained in it—that moral law which it so much concerns us to know and to observe—but also because of its doctrines upon which our faith is founded, and its promises by which our hope is animated. The universal recognition of the Bible in our Lodges, and its use as a masonic symbol, teach us that it behoves us to be truly religious, and earnest in religion, not contented with merely acknowledging the existence of God, but living in a continual recognition of this great truth, fearing, loving, and serving God. We are thus also taught to be thankful to Him for the revelation which He has graciously made to us, a revelation of Himself,

by which we attain a far more perfect knowledge of Him
than we could obtain by the mere light of nature, although
the heavens declare His glory, and the firmament showeth
His handy-work; a revelation of ourselves, by which we
learn the very secrets of our own hearts, with all their
corruption, and all their liability to temptation, far more
thoroughly than we otherwise could, our hearts ever
responding to the declarations which God's Word contains
and assenting to their truth; a revelation of our relation to
God both as a God of justice and a God of mercy; a
revelation of the way in which He has appointed that we
should seek Him, in order to obtain mercy and to enjoy His
favour; a revelation concerning the future, radiant with the
promise of a resurrection from the dead, and a blissful
immortality.   We are taught that it behoves us strictly to
observe the moral law, in every part and commandment of
it, because every transgression of it is an offence against the
majesty of Heaven, and wilful transgression of it implies
contempt of Him whom we ought to fear and love and serve,
contempt of His wisdom, of His power, of His holiness,
and of all His attributes.   No good man can be a wilful
and habitual transgressor of any commandment of the
moral law; and nothing can be imagined more contrary to
the character of a good and worthy mason.

It were easy to write volumes in praise of the Bible,
without exhausting the theme; but it is not easy to find words
in which duly to set forth its claims to our admiration,
reverence, and esteem.   In no other book, nor in all other
books put together, do we find such a view of human
history, traced from the very creation of man, and carried
on partly as a record of events which have taken place,
partly in prophecy, to the consummation of all things, in
"the day of God wherein the heavens being on fire shall
be dissolved, and the elements shall melt with fervent
heat," but the righteous shall enter into the enjoyment of
"new heavens and a new earth" (2 Pet. iii. 12, 13).   The
doctrines of the Bible are so glorious and excellent, that by
their very nature they compel us to regard them as no mere

invention or production of the human mind, but as coming to us from a higher source. What a contrast does the doctrine of the unity of God present to that of any form of heathenism! How sublime the truth that "Our God made the heavens!" What a contrast do we find in the view given us in the Bible of the divine attributes, to the character of any of the heathen divinities, whether of classic or barbarous mythology!. Again, how wonderful the whole system of doctrine contained in the Bible! how admirably adapted to the attributes of God on the one hand, and on the other hand to the nature and wants of man! How admirable it all is in this one all-pervading characteristic, that it exalts God and not man, assigning to man the place of a mere dependant on God's bounty, grace, and mercy! False religions differ essentially in this respect from the religion taught in the Bible; and every corruption of the religion of the Bible is a return to one of the essential principles of heathenism, the exaltation of man as capable of atoning for his own sins, and winning for himself the favour of God, by sacrifices, by self-inflicted tortures, by alms-giving, by good works; this theoretical exaltation all the while implying and resulting in a real degradation, whilst the Bible principle which exalts God and ascribes all to His grace, tends to purify and ennoble every one who receives it, and lives under the power of it. Further, what an inexhaustible subject of admiration is presented to us in the moral teaching of the Bible, in its brief summations of the moral law, and in the multitude of lessons by which that law is expounded and enforced, in history, in proverbs, in didactic discourses, in sacred songs, in parables! Was ever lesson of charity so impressive as the Parable of the Good Samaritan? Was ever charity so beautifully depicted and so eloquently extolled, as in the thirteenth chapter of the First Epistle to the Corinthians? Who can read that chapter, and not be constrained to acknowledge that its author was inspired? But every page of the Bible contains evidence of its inspiration. There is no eloquence like that of the Bible, no poetry like that of the Bible, poetry simple enough for a child, and yet sublime to a degree far exceeding that of any other volume that ever won the admiration of men.

It is wonderful how little many, even of those who unhesitatingly profess to receive the Bible as the Word of God, and therefore to accept it as the rule of their faith and of their life, seem to consider or appreciate what may be called its literary excellence. And yet this excellence is so transcendent, the books of the Bible are so superior in this respect to all other books, that from this alone it may be confidently inferred that they are not mere human compositions, the productions of unaided human authorship. Let us look, for example, at the poetry of the Bible. Some books of the Old Testament consist entirely, others chiefly of poetry. The book of Psalms and the Song of Solomon contain nothing else; the books of the prophets and the book of Job contain only a few passages of prose, the prophecies themselves being all in the form of poetry. And although Hebrew versification is very imperfectly understood, even by Hebrew scholars, and those who are not Hebrew scholars lie under the disadvantage of reading the poetry of the Bible only in translations, yet any one who reads it with a mind attentive to its sublimity and beauty, must be constrained to acknowledge that in these respects many passages surpass the most admirable passages of all the poets, either of ancient or of modern times. Nor can this be explained by mere reference to the grandeur of the themes of which it treats, the excellence of the truths which it embodies, and what may be deemed their natural power to affect the heart. In fact, the themes of the poet are difficult in proportion to their very grandeur; the grandest themes are always the most difficult, and require genius of the highest order for their suitable treatment. Religious poetry has always been regarded as more difficult than poetry of any other description; and the very necessity of embodying or strictly adhering to religious truth has been supposed by some writers of high reputation in the department of *belles lettres*, to lay a restraint on the imagination, such as to make the production of religious poetry of a high

order impossible, or almost impossible. To this opinion we
do not subscribe, and there are many poems both in our
own and other languages, a reference to which is a sufficient
refutation of it. But its most complete refutation is
afforded by the poetry of the Bible itself. How sublime
the imagery in some passages, how exquisitely beautiful in
others ! Were we to begin to quote examples, we would
soon exceed the limits to which we desire to restrict
ourselves, and it would be but a very imperfect view of the
subject which a few illustrative examples could afford.
But we may be allowed to direct attention to the
twenty-third psalm, as an example of great and most
important religious truths conveyed in simple words, and
of deep and blissful religious feeling expressed also with
the most perfect simplicity, and by the use of imagery of
the most natural kind, the Lord's care of His people and
bounty towards them being represented as the care of a
shepherd in providing for his flock, and of a beneficent host
abundantly supplying all the wants of his guests. Can
anything exceed in sublimity the opening verses of the
139th psalm, which declare the omniscience and omni-
presence of God, and the impossibility of escaping from His
eye and from His power? How admirable even as a mere
picture of the aspect of nature when winter passes into
spring, and the heart of man rejoices in the new sweetness
and beauty of the most delightful season of the year, are
these verses of the Song of Solomon!—" My beloved spake,
and said unto me, Rise up, my love, my fair one, and come
away : For lo, the winter is past, the rain is over and gone ;
the flowers appear on the earth ; the time of the singing of
birds is come, and the voice of the turtle is heard in our
land ; the fig-tree putteth forth her green figs, and the
vines with the tender grapes give a good smell : Arise, my
love, my fair one, and come away " (Song of Solomon ii.
10–13). And yet how much is the beauty of the poetry
enhanced in our estimation, when we consider the spiritual
meaning of these verses, and view them as declaring the
Lord's love to His people and delight in His church ! Very

different in its character is that passage of the fourteenth
chapter of Isaiah, concerning the destruction of Babylon
(Isa. xiv. 4–27), which has been regarded, and not without
strong reason, as the most sublime passage of poetry in
any book or language. In variety of the imagery, in
strength of expression, in terribleness of denunciation, it
may well be said to be absolutely unparalleled. " Hell *
from beneath is moved for thee to meet thee at thy coming,"
the prophet says, and adds image to image throughout
many verses, all in keeping with this leading idea, and yet
wonderfully various. How striking, impressive, and
terrible, is the description of a predicted famine in the
fourteenth chapter of Jeremiah! How many remarkable
features are combined in these few verses! " Judah
mourneth, and the gates thereof languish; they are black
unto the ground, and the cry of Jerusalem is gone up.
And their nobles have sent their little ones unto the waters;
they came to the pits, and found no water, they returned
with their vessels empty; they were ashamed and confounded
and covered their heads. Because the ground is chapt,
for there was no rain in the earth, the plowmen were
ashamed, they covered their heads. Yea, the hind calved in
the field, and forsook it, because there was no grass. And
the wild asses did stand in the high places, they snuffed up
the wind like dragons: their eyes did fail, because there
was no grass" (Jer. xiv. 2–6). Inanimate and animate nature
are both brought into requisition here, the sufferings of the
beasts are represented as well as those of man, and that
the calamity is one felt by the rich as much as by
the poor is made strongly to appear by the mention of the
daughters of the nobles as going to the pits for water, and
going in vain.

To one other passage alone shall we refer, ere passing from
this subject,—the description of a vision put into the mouth
of Eliphaz, the Temanite, in the Book of Job. " In thoughts
from visions of the night, when deep sleep falleth on
men, Fear came upon me, and trembling, which made all

* *Hades*, the place of the dead.

my bones to shake. Then a spirit passed before my face; the hair of my flesh stood up: It stood still, but I could not discern the form thereof: an image was before mine eyes, there was silence, and I heard a voice saying, Shall mortal man be more just than God? shall a man be more pure than his Maker?" (Job iv. 13–17.) Surely it must be readily admitted that this is a passage of admirable sublimity. All the literature of the world may be searched in vain for a parallel to it.

It is to be observed also that all the poems of the Bible are complete and finished poems. Poetic thought and feeling are often expressed even by authors of considerable distinction, in very agreeable verses, whilst yet the so-called poem produced is not a poem in a proper sense; it has no very definite purpose, no leading thought to which all else is subordinate. But it is never so in the Bible. The writer always shows that he has a purpose, and everything perfectly accords with it. Each poem is thoroughly complete and finished; no imperfection appears in the execution of the purpose intended. Look again, for example, to the Twenty-third Psalm. The key-note is struck in the first verse, " The Lord is my Shepherd, I shall not want." Then follow verses expressive of the blessedness enjoyed under this Shepherd's care, from His infinite wisdom, power, and love; and the first part of the psalm appropriately ends with that expression of unbounded confidence and hope, " Yea, though I walk through the valley of the shadow of death, I will fear no evil, for Thou art with me, Thy rod and Thy staff they comfort me." Again the same strain is resumed in the second part, under the new figure of a host bountifully providing for his guest, and the psalm ends with a general expression of confidence and hope, similar to that which concludes the first part, but more general, and extending to the whole future of time and eternity: " Surely goodness and mercy shall follow me all the days of my life, and I will dwell in the house of the Lord for ever." It is thus with every other psalm of the whole 150, it is thus with every poem in the Bible. The Song of Solomon is comparatively a long poem; but its structure is as worthy of admiration as the poetic beauty of any particular passage.

But as the Scriptures excel in poetry, they display a similar superiority and perfection in every form of prose composition. The style of the historic and didactic portions is remarkable for its simplicity.

There is not one sentence that approaches in the slightest degree to the character of turgidity or bombast, and yet the historic narratives are extremely clear; scenes and events are most vividly and graphically depicted. Conversations are recorded in such a manner as to add to the interest of the narrative, to bring out strongly the nature of the recorded events, and to exhibit most strikingly the characters of the persons concerned in them. Some of the persons of whom our knowledge is derived only from Scripture history, seem to live before us more perfectly than any of whom we read in any other histories or biographies. It is hardly necessary to allude to the accounts given in the four gospels of the life and ministry of our Lord Jesus Christ. But even subordinate characters that appear only once and pass away from our view, are exhibited in a vivid distinctness of portraiture, beyond what even the most highly-gifted authors have been able to attain to in their works.

Again, we find in Scripture, and notably in the writings of the Apostle Paul, many passages of the noblest argumentative eloquence, close reasoning on the most solemn and important of themes, accompanied with continual and powerful application to the conscience and heart. In expostulatory, hortative, and persuasive passages, we find at one time the strong expression of righteous indignation, at another the most affectionate and pathetic pleading, the most solemn warning, or the most cheering words of encouragement. Two passages may be specially referred to, out of the multitude which readily present themselves, as affording examples of the holy eloquence and sublimity of Scripture; the concluding portion of the eighth chapter of the Epistle of Paul to the Romans, and the fifteenth chapter of the First Epistle of the same Apostle to the Corinthians. In the former of these passages, we find the apostle summing up a long argument, and at the same time speaking, not as one whose province it was merely to argue and convince by argument, but as one commissioned by God and by His authority declaring the great things of the kingdom of heaven. The triumph of faith which the concluding verses express, reaches the highest degree of sublimity. And so it is in the fifteenth chapter of the First Epistle to the Corinthians. The resurrection of the dead is declared with divine authority, as a truth that may not be questioned; its connection with the other truths of religion, and the whole scheme of salvation is demonstrated; the gainsayer is met on his own ground and confuted; the glory and blessedness of the resurrection are set forth in a few striking sentences, and then comes the sublime and triumphant conclusion, the apostle expressing his own joy in which every believer is called to partake with him. " So when this corruptible shall have put on incorruption, and this mortal shall have put on immortality, then shall be brought to pass the saying that is written, Death is swallowed up in victory. O death, where is thy sting? O grave, where is thy victory? The sting of death is sin; and the strength of sin is the law. But thanks be to God, which giveth us the victory, through our Lord Jesus Christ " (1 Cor. xv. 54–57).

All these things being considered, can we wonder that the translation of the Bible into the languages of modern Europe, and especially into English and German, has had more effect than all other causes in the creation of their literature, and in giving it the form and character which it has ever since borne? The English language has been fixed by the translation of the Bible to a degree that it probably never otherwise would have been; very few of the words used in the authorised version, although it is not very far from three hundred years old, have become obsolete or have materially charged in their signification. As to the German language, it was Luther's translation of the Bible which first made one of its dialects classic, the common language of literature and of the whole German people. The modern language of Germany owes its present form in a great measure to this one great and permanent work. And the whole character of literature, both in this country and in Germany, has been affected to a degree beyond all possibility of estimation, by the general circulation and reading of the Holy Scriptures.

It remains to be pointed out, as a distinguishing characteristic of the Bible, that the sins and errors even of those who are generally presented as examples of piety and virtue, are not concealed, but faithfully recorded. This accords well with the idea that the Bible histories are inspired records, and with the great purpose for which the whole Bible must be considered as having been written—the religious instruction and spiritual good of man. But every one knows how contrary it is to the ordinary manner of men, to the practice of human biographers, who continually conceal or palliate faults, making the saint too perfect in holiness, or representing the life of a good man as one unwearied and unvaried course of virtue. How much men need the warning to be found in the Scripture record of the sins of Abraham, and Moses, and David, and Peter, and others ; how much they need the encouragement afforded by the record of their repentance and pardon, we need not stay to show.

We must yet add as a fact, in which, perhaps, more than even in any other, the excellency of Scripture appears, that its meaning can never be fully searched out and exhausted. There are depths which we cannot fathom, heights which we cannot scale. Read it as often as you may, there are still new meanings to be found in the most familiar passages. New riches may always be found in that mine, fresh water in that well. Those who have studied the Scriptures longest and most diligently, are always most fully sensible of the imperfection of their own acquaintance with them. And from this alone, it might be confidently agreed that the Bible is the Word of God. For it is not thus with

ordinary human productions, but it is thus with all the
works of God. We may read and study any work of mere
human genius, till we have so thoroughly mastered it, that
we can no longer expect to find in it anything new. We
may examine the mechanism of a watch or a steam-engine,
till we know all about it as well as the maker himself;
but we cannot so exhaust by study any work of God. The
grand system of the Universe is ever displaying new
wonders to the astronomer; the chemist makes new discoveries every day concerning the elements of nature and
their manifold combinations; we cannot say of a single
plant or animal, a single leaf or flower, a single eye or
wing of an insect, that we have learned all that is to be
learned, and know all that can be known about it. No
wise man supposes that all can ever be found out. The
correspondence, in this respect, between the Holy Scriptures
and the works of God shows them to be of the same
authorship.

It does not belong to our purpose or province here to maintain an argument in favour of inspiration, far less to attempt
to define its nature, or to show how it consists with that
variety of style which appears in the different books of
Scripture, according, it would seem, to the natural bent of
the minds of those who wrote them as they were directed
and guided by God. But we cannot refrain from remarking,
that in following out the trains of thought which have been
suggested in the preceding pages, valuable materials will
be found for argument in favour of the inspiration of the
Bible, and in support of its claim to be received as the
Word of God.

It is because the Bible is and has ever been received and
esteemed as the Great Light of Freemasonry, that Freemasonry has flourished throughout so many ages, and that
it still continues to flourish with all the vigour and beauty
of youth, full of hope and promise for times still to come.
When we behold this great masonic symbol, let our hearts
be filled with awe, with gratitude, and with hope.

O

CPSIA information can be obtained
at www.ICGtesting.com
Printed in the USA
LVIC06n1812230718
584660LV00008B/88

CARNIVOROUS PLANTS
CARE AND CULTIVATION

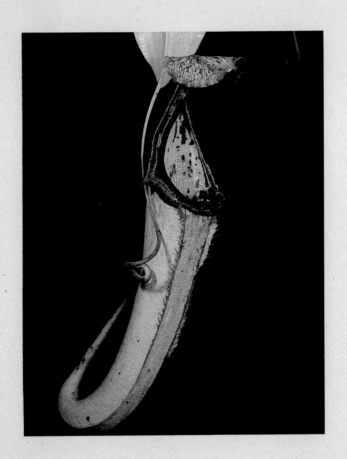

CARNIVOROUS PLANTS
CARE AND CULTIVATION

Marcel Lecoufle

FOREWORD BY
JEAN-MARIE PELT

CASSELL

The photograph on the half-title page shows *Nepenthes × deslogesii*, a trap or urn form of plant, about to capture a bumblebee.

Facing the title page is *Sarracenia × catesbaei*, showing its traps and flower.

Illustration p. 9: *Drosera capensis* (Cape sundew). Midges are stuck to the tentacles.

Illustration p. 49: *Nepenthes masoalensis*. A climber, in its natural habitat, north-east Madagascar.

Cassell Publishers Limited
Villiers House, 41/47 Strand
London WC2N 5JE

First published in the United Kingdom. 1990
This edition 1993
English text copyright © Cassell Publishers Ltd. 1990

World copyright © 1989 Bordas S.A. 11 Rue Gossin, 92543 Montrouge, France

Distributed in the United States by
Sterling Publishing Co. Inc
387 Park Avenue South, New York, N.Y. 10016-8810

Distributed in Australia by
Capricorn Link (Australia) Pty Ltd
P.O. Box 665, Lane Cove, NSW 2066

British Library Cataloguing in Publication Data
Lecoufle, Marcel
    Carnivorous plants.
    1.   Carnivorous plants. Cultivation
    I. Title II. Comment choisir et cultiver vos plantes carnivores. *English*
    635

ISBN 0-304-34330-7

English translation: J. P. Farrar
Edited for this edition by: Paul Temple and Roy Gasson

Line drawings: Danièle Molez

All photographs by the author except: © Robert Cantley (page 13 and page 133 top left); © Lorenz Bütschi (pages 40 and 99); © Bruce Lee Bednar (pages 102 and 105); © Anne-Marie Dey (page 129).

Typeset by Litho Link Ltd, Welshpool, Powys, Wales
Printed and bound by New Interlitho, Trezzano (Milan), Italy

CONTENTS

PART TWO   TRAPS AND FLOWERS

Drosera capensis (Cape sundew). The plant has captured and is digesting a large spider as well as (right) a smaller victim.

Foreword

For botanists and orchid lovers the world over, as well as for nature lovers and enthusiasts, the name of Marcel Lecoufle is associated with orchids, that immense family of plants that are so expert at making insects the accomplices of their pollination. And orchids, like carnivorous plants, use trickery to attract insects. The difference is that carnivorous plants use insects to ensure not only pollination but also the plant's very existence.

There are, therefore, plants that entrust insects with two different missions. The first, quite ordinary, task is pollination – nearly 200,000 plants, that is 70 per cent to 80 per cent of those that bear flowers, are pollinated by insects. The second, much more specific one, aims to make a prey of insects, thereby ensuring the plant's nourishment in soils or terrain generally poor in nutrients. Plants that feed on insects in this way are the true carnivores (it would perhaps be more accurate to say insectivores). They form a club of some 530 species living naturally throughout the world and divided into 15 genera and 7 families. This list, though, is by no means exhaustive – new carnivorous species are still being discovered, such as, very recently, the Bromeliads (Bromeliaceae) of the forests of Venezuela.

A number of plants of this large American family have leaves that overlap at the base to form a jar that collects rainwater running down the limb. This is a technique by which plants perched on trees and with underdeveloped roots ensure themselves a supply of water. Insects frequently come to drink at this natural water tank and end up drowning in it. One species, *Brocchinia reducta*, the latest carnivorous plant to be discovered, has devised a way of taking advantage of these accidents. It produces a secretion that digests the insects after bacteria have transformed them and made them easier to absorb. This is an evolutionary direction that had not been credited to the Bromeliads and which suggests the possibility of other similar discoveries. Insects had already been trapped by the very nature of the plant's organization and by its method of water collection; it was only necessary to go a little further and to devise a means of assimilating the prey.

Other discoveries will doubtless follow and one can understand why the number of listed carnivorous species never ceases to grow – twenty or so years ago only 450 species were known. To today's list one could add also the 140 species of carnivorous, microscopic fungi, which deploy the most ingenious traps in the soil in order to catch for example

nematodes, worms that destroy roots. Some of these fungi use a gluey substance to entrap their prey. Others use snares – just as the carnivorous Bromeliads transformed their water jars into digestive tubes, so these fungi have transformed their filaments into slipknots.

Remarkably, the traps of carnivorous plants are usually the leaves or some other specialized organ (the urns of the *Nepenthes*, for example, or the bladders of the *Utricularia*), never the flowers. No carnivorous plant has a carnivorous flower or a trap that results from an adaptation or modification of its flowers. There is a perfect allocation of tasks – the flower is pollinated by insects specifically linked to it while the trap organs capture other insects, usually of a great variety, to feed the plant. It is not, of course, impossible that we may one day discover a carnivorous flower that will possess the dual function of reproduction and feeding, but it seems improbable.

Carnivorous plants are astonishing also in that they are distributed through numerous groups of plants that are not botanically related. This must mean that the change to a carnivorous stage is not a phenomenon that might have occurred once during the course of evolution and passed down through the lineage of a plant. On the contrary, the dispersal of carnivores throughout the 250,000 species of higher plants shows that changeovers to this method of feeding occurred a number of times, engendering several clearly distinguishable evolutionary lines. The most modest category is without doubt the *Cephalotus*, represented by a single species that is a family in its own right – the Cephalotaceae, modestly confined to the outskirts of the Australian town of Albany. At the opposite end of the scale, other groups are made up of large numbers – like the *Drosera* with their hundred or so species and the *Utricularia* with 275 species. These two genera are represented on all five continents, with a preference nevertheless for Australia, a country richly endowed with carnivorous plants.

Carnivorous plants are so accustomed to living off their prey that they turn up their noses at food offered as replacement. They dissociate themselves from the normal feeding habits of plants that gain their nourishment from the soil via the roots. They are so successful that they can survive in areas particularly poor in nutrients, especially nitrogen, where more orthodox plants would die of malnutrition.

Given their specialized food demands, the cultivation of carnivorous plants poses some problems. The reader will find

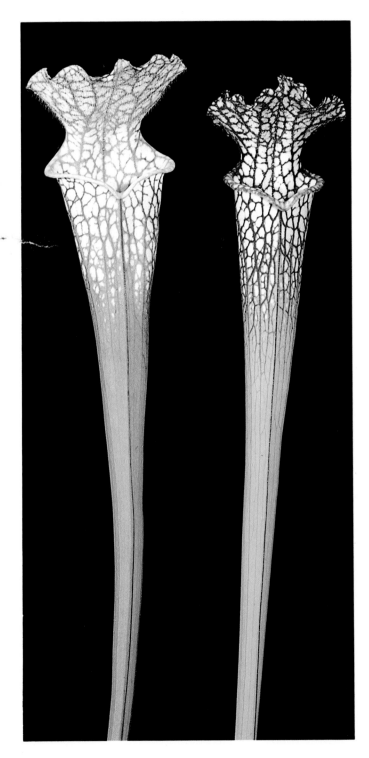

in this book instructions and advice for the cultivation of each species.

Some plants have travelled only partway along the road to being truly carnivorous. Take, for example, two species of *Roridula* that grow spontaneously on the outskirts of Cape Town in South Africa and which form on their own a small, very unusual family. These plants possess glandular hairs like the *Drosera* but have no digestive glands capable of absorbing prey, so they cannot feed themselves – to the great benefit of spiders, who are provided with a ready captured food supply. The *Roridula* have set off on the carnivorous route but have not yet come to the end; in a few thousand years evolution may make them true carnivores, but for the moment, they are content to hunt prey for others.

The French peat-bog *Drosera*, although protected today, have paid a heavy price to the pharmaceutical industry because of the over-zealous harvesting of their digestive leaves, which provide an extract used medicinally as an expectorant. The digestive liquid of the *Nepenthes*, found in the bottom of their urns, was used for treating incontinence – taken orally and also sprinkled on the head of the patient. In the large urns situated at their leaf-ends the *Nepenthes* have turned the digestion of prey into a fine art, through the combined action of bacteria and enzymes, which they accommodate and secrete in the same way as do humans in their intestines. The *Nepenthes* are supposed also to relieve pain and distress – their name is from a Greek word meaning banisher of grief.

It is in the art of capturing prey by the use of rapidly moving traps that the carnivores distinguish themselves most from the generally accepted idea of plants, whose immobility and fixed, supported state are their two traditionally distinctive features.

We find in the carnivores very precise, rapid, and often sophisticated capture mechanisms. The *Dionaea* or the *Aldrovanda* have leaves in the form of steel traps, consisting of two toothed lobes capable of closing upon each other by folding along their central axis and interlocking their teeth. Closure takes place in 1/30s in the *Dionea* and at the amazing speed of 1/1000s in the *Aldrovanda*. The aquatic urns of the bladderworts inflate suddenly in order to suck in both water and prey; the

Sarracenia leucophylla (White trumpet). The traps or trumpets of one of the carnivorous plant species living in a natural state in the world.

movement takes only $^1/_{500}$s. Glue traps, on the contrary, move slowly, like the leaves of *Drosera* or *Pinguicula*. Other carnivores lack movement but are no less subtle. They have trumpets, pitchers, or flaps into which the insect penetrates easily but is then inexorably held prisoner by hair collars or insurmountable ridges. From this point of view, carnivorous plants offer the physiologist almost totally unexplored territory since, strange as it may seem, we know almost nothing about spontaneous plant movement. We have, at best, simply noted it. Having for generations been certain that no system for transmitting information existed within the vegetable world, researchers have simply turned a blind eye to sporadic observations that seem, disturbingly, to indicate that something akin to information transfer is taking place. Those who work in the large greenhouses of botanic gardens are aware that many plants close their leaves in the evening and open them in the morning. We also know that certain flowers are capable of opening at a surprising speed, their corollas bursting open in a few seconds, and that the tension within the *Ecballium* makes them eject their seeds at amazing speed.

There is no doubt, however, that the carnivorous plants hold their best surprises for those who observe carefully and with sophistication their methods of capturing prey. Their contribution is to give the plant world a lifelike character through behaviour which sometimes resembles that of the animal world and which thereby brings them closer to us. Despite their apparent immobility, we can place them more readily in the living world, of which they form a distinct part.

Today, carnivorous plants are enjoying a revival in popular interest. The traps and the cunning and sophisticated strategies they have invented cannot leave us indifferent, since the behaviour and manners they display are also our own. Raising orchids at home implies a knowledge of certain tricks of the trade that are vital to their well-being. It is the same for carnivorous plants: it would be quite wrong to cultivate them in an ordinary flower pot without taking due care to select the appropriate soil and the correct treatment.

Marcel Lecoufle explains all this to us. Reading his remarkable work on carnivorous plants, we discover one part of the immense botanical world that we still only half understand – the world that those who love nature and plants, in other words each one of us, wishes to discover further, and thereby love all the more!

JEAN-MARIE PELT

Professor of Plant Biology, University of Metz

President of the European Institute of Ecology

Note on nomenclature

The carnivorous plants dealt with in detail in this book (pp.49 to 137), are given firstly their scientific (Latin) names, followed by their common names (where they exist). This usage is based on current practice – carnivorous plants are generally sold under their Latin names. It also allows us to cite all species, not all of which possess a common name, and avoids any risk of confusion – Latin names are completely universal. The best-known species under cultivation are dealt with in detail (*see* Part Three).

To find a plant not mentioned in Part Three, the reader should refer to species and hybrids listed in pages 138 to 142, and, where they exist, species and their hybrids are classified according to their genus. The genera *Drosera* and *Pinguicula* have, in addition, been classified according to their various botanical characteristics and methods of cultivation. These lists will enable the less common varieties to be linked to the species explained in detail in the body of the work.

Part One
GENERAL PRINCIPLES

Carnivorous plants – an introduction

Longitudinal section of a trap (or urn) of *Nepenthes*. In the lower part can be seen the remains of digested ants; × 1.6.

Definition and limitations

Both mysterious and fascinating, the carnivores are plants that have acquired, in the course of evolution, the remarkable ability to attract, capture, and digest living animal prey. Since the plant world is everywhere else the source of food for numerous animals, this ability is a kind of revenge.

The animals caught by carnivorous plants are mostly various kinds of insects – midges, ants, flies, wasps, and cockroaches – and this is why we sometimes use the term insectivorous plants. Other small invertebrates may also be trapped, however. The size of the victim is, naturally, dependent upon the size of the plant – while the more modest carnivores are content with amoebas and other microscopic organisms, the largest are sometimes capable of digesting a small mammal or bird.

Strictly speaking, carnivorousness is a state that implies for the plant not only the ability to capture animals but also to digest them. This excludes from our discussion species such as those of the genus *Roridula* (*R. muscicapa*), native to South Africa. These plants, which may be termed semi-insectivorous, have all the requirements for capturing insects and, in particular, they have glandular hairs, like the *Drosera*. However, they do not possess digestive glands and they are therefore incapable of digesting their prey.

For the record, we should also cite the myrmecophiles, which do not capture live prey but exist in symbiosis with ants. The ants feed at the expense of the plant, which in return benefits from their excreta and dead bodies. Myremecophile plants are easily cultivated under glass in the presence of ants. Then there are the carnivorous fungi, whose biology is too special for them to be considered with standard carnivorous plants; they capture small nematode worms in the soil with the aid of organs situated on their mycelium. The cultivation of carnivorous fungi is a very delicate operation.

Finally, we should mention the genus *Brocchinia*, of the Bromeliaceae family, one species of which (*B. reducta*) has been considered carnivorous since 1984. This plant can be found in its natural state in Venezuela and Guyana at altitudes over 3000ft (1000m), in areas of full sunlight. The leaves of *B. reducta* are erect and form a tight rosette. Insects drown in the water at the heart of the plant and are then assimilated by bacteria.

Carnivorous plants and the plant kingdom

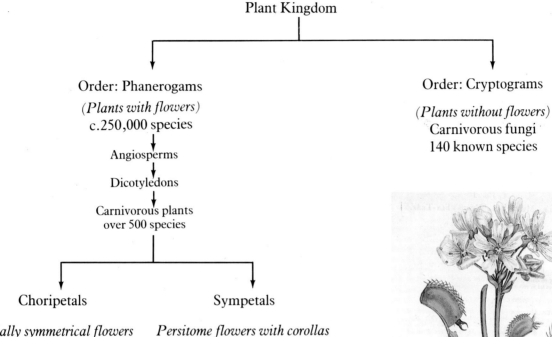

Plant Kingdom

Order: Phanerogams

(Plants with flowers)
c.250,000 species

↓

Angiosperms

↓

Dicotyledons

↓

Carnivorous plants
over 500 species

Order: Cryptograms

(Plants without flowers)
Carnivorous fungi
140 known species

Choripetals

*Radially symmetrical flowers
with independent
petals growing from
the centre*

Families

Biblidaceae
Cephalotaceae
Dioncophyllaceae
Droseraceae
Nepenthaceae
Sarraceniaceae

Sympetals

*Persitome flowers with corollas
in the form of a mask with two
lips and whose throat is closed
by a projection or palate*

Family

Lentibulariaceae

Plate taken from the review *Curtis's
Botanical Magazine* (vol. XX)
showing the Venus (*Dionaea
muscipula*) of the Droseraceae
family; × 0.5.

Basic biological principles

Carnivorous plants and the plant kingdom

The carnivorous plants comprise more than 500 species growing naturally; they are grouped into 7 families. They are all phanerogams (plants with flowers). They are also mostly dictotyledonous angiosperms.

There is a large morphological diversity in the carnivorous

Common butterwort (*Pinguicula vulgaris*) of the Lentibulariaceae family, in its natural
habitat in France. It is the leaves that form the traps.

plants. Their size varies according to the species, from a fraction of an inch (a few millimetres) in the smallest to over 60 ft (20 metres) in the largest, which develop as climbing vines. Depending on the habitat, polymorphism may also exist within the same species. This is the case with *Nepenthes vieillardii* (Nepenthaceae family), a carnivorous plant found in New Caledonia from sea level, where the minimum temperature is about 16°C, to 3500ft (1100m), where the thermometer sometimes drops to freezing point.

The flowers are equally variable between genera. They often have a brief life, but stand above the surrounding vegetation on their stalks and prove most efficient at attracting insects. The flowers of carnivorous plants bear no capture mechanism, this function being the sole prerogative of the traps. Their raison d'être, as with the other flowering plants, is multiplication and thus the survival of the species.

A group of *Drosera neo-caledonica*, a species of Droseraceae endemic to New Caledonia. The leaves have gland-tipped tentacles of vivid red that attract, then capture, insects. These provide a nutritional supplement to the plants' diet, allowing them to survive on this poor substratum, of volcanic origin.

Why carnivorous plants?

Why have some plant species, often biologically quite distinct from each other, developed this extraordinary property called carnivorousness. In order to grow and reproduce, plants require certain essential elements – oxygen, carbon dioxide, water, various mineral salts (principally constituents of nitrogen, calcium, potassium, and phosphorus) – as well as vitamins and hormones. To satisfy these needs, plants have perfected strategies related to the very varied environments that they have been able to colonize.

In particular, we often find carnivorous plants growing in acid soils (peat bogs) or in acid waters that are poor in mineral salts. In order to survive in these impoverished habitats, the carnivorous plants have devised traps that are the result of several thousand years of evolution. The prey captured and assimilated by these traps supply vitamins and proteins that plants living in richer soils take in through their roots in the form of mineral salts. Experiments with carnivorous plants have shown that fertilizers of whatever sort can in no way

replace the nutrition contributed by the captured insects, if one wants to obtain vigorous, flowering plants.

Carnivorous plants and man

History

The first botanists to study the carnivores noted that they captured insects but did not realize that they could extract a part of their nourishment from them. It was Dobbs, governor of North Carolina, who, in about 1760, was the first to apply the term carnivorous plant to the Venus flytrap (genus *Dionaea*). At around the same time, the *Encyclopédie* of Diderot and d'Alembert discussed the Venus flytrap and species of the genera *Utricularia*, *Drosera*, and *Pinguicula*.

In about 1865 Charles Darwin demonstrated by experiment the carnivorous nature of insectivorous plants; his work, *Insectivorous Plants*, published in 1877, remains even today a standard reference. Darwin thought the Venus flytrap to be 'the most extraordinary plant in the world'.

For some decades, carnivorous plants have been a subject of passionate interest among numerous amateurs – there are now more genera in artificial cultivation than there are in their natural habitats, which are often fragile, threatened sites.

Mythology and beliefs

Carnivorous plants have been the source of many legends. If a young bird or small rabbit can be digested in the urn of a *Nepenthes*, why cannot a carnivorous plant be capable of capturing a man? A number of books, based on the accounts of explorers who cared little for scientific truth, have developed this theme. Thus, at the end of the last century, there was talk of the 'man-eating tree of Madagascar', as terrifying as it was mythical.

Medicinal properties and special uses

Ancient botanical treatises and pharmacopoeias attribute various properties to the sundews, or *Drosera*, whose red droplets of mucilage do not dry out in the sun. Certain extracts of these plants serve as treatment for corns, verrucas, and burns. Infusions and other extracts were used against coughs, respiratory disorders, tuberculosis, arteriosclerosis, inflammations, intestinal illnesses, and syphilis. These preparations were diuretic, soothing, and even aphrodisiac. Today, extracts

Urn of a natural hybrid of *Nepenthes rafflesiana* and *N. bicalcarata*. The huge size of the urn allows large prey to be captured.

of *Drosera* are still used against coughs and ailments of the respiratory tract. The large-leaved butterwort, or *Pinguicula*, was used to treat wounds. It was, and is, also used in the production of various cheeses – its leaves can, because of their high acidity, curdle milk.

The natives of certain tropical regions dare not, even today, touch *Nepenthes*, fearing the evil powers the plants are supposed to possess. *Nepenthes* are, though, used medicinally in a variety of ways. The liquid contained in the young urns before the operculum opens is an astringent and it seems also to have the property of soothing sore throats, inflammations, and disorders of the skin and eyes. According to Homer, it relieves sorrow and grief. Extracts of the boiled roots have been used against dysentery and stomach complaints and the whole plant is used in various homeopathic preparations.

Families and genera

Carnivorous plants, as it has been said, consist of 7 families, of which 6 are major ones. These are made up of some 15 genera and about 530 species, living in the wild throughout the world. These figures do not take into account those fungi which are able to capture insects.

Cephalotus follicularis, the only species of the Cephalotaceae family. The rosette of leaves can be seen, surrounded by the traps; × 1.8.

The world of carnivorous plants

Family	Principal genera	Number of species
Byblidaceae	*Byblis*	2
Cephalotaceae	*Cephalotus*	1
Droseraceae	*Aldrovanda*	1
	Dionaea	1
	Drosera	100
	Drosophyllum	1
Lentibulariaceae	*Biovularia*	2
	Genlisea	16
	Pinguicula	>50
	Polypompholyx	2
	Utricularia	275
Nepenthaceae	*Nepenthes*	72
Sarraceniaceae	*Heliamphora*	5
	Sarracenia	9
	Darlingtonia	1

In this chapter the main characteristics of each family of carnivorous plants are described. Then the principal genera are discussed, with the emphasis upon the more numerous species, and finally the genera that are not at present commercially available or cultivated are dealt with.

Byblidaceae

The Byblidaceae family is made up of the single genus *Byblis*, which comprises only two species, *B. gigantea* and *B. liniflora*. These plants, of Australian origin, give the appearance in the adult stage of small bushes; they have a very hard rhizome from which the stems grow. These are renewed each year after the dry season. The rhizomes allow the plants to survive after bush fires have destroyed the parts above ground. Their leaves, alternate, linear, and with a broad base, are almost triangular in section. They are covered with glandular hairs, having a large quantity of mucilage which sparkles in the sun. The immobile hairs decorate all parts of the plant, from the stem right up to the flower sepals. Where they grow naturally, the myriad sparkling drops viewed against the sun break up the light into many colours.

As well as the hairs, responsible for capturing prey, the Byblidaceae have very small digestive glands arranged in lines on each side of the leaves and on the stems. The flowers, violet in colour, are very numerous and borne by the stalks starting at the base of each leaf. It is the flowers that principally distinguish the *Byblis* from another genus of carnivorous plants, the *Drosera* – in all other respects the two genera show a close morphological resemblance.

Cephalotaceae

Cephalotus follicularis is the only species of the Cephalotaceae family. This plant's habitat is restricted to the surroundings of the Australian town of Albany. In winter it forms a rosette of oblong leaves; in summer these develop into the pitchers or urns that constitute the traps. The leaves are numerous but small. An underground rhizome allows the plant to survive brush fires or very low temperatures. Since in its natural state it lives surrounded by long grasses, *C. follicularis* is a species that prefers some shade.

Droseraceae

Most of the Droseraceae (from the Greek *drosos*, dew) are hardy perennials. In winter they form bulbs or buds and in spring produce new shoots from these or from seeds sown naturally around the mother plants. Plants of this family grow, according to the species, to anything between a fraction of an inch (a few millimetres) and 2 ft (60 cm) in height. The leaves that form the traps are often borne in rosette formation. The trap, which may be either thread-like or disc-shaped, can move and is covered with glandular hairs, each of which has at its extremity a drop of mucilage, shining in the light. The flowers are hermaphrodite; they have five petals, between four and twenty stamens, and an ovary of one to five compartments. The capsule-shaped fruit contains numerous black seeds with a fleshy albumen.

The Droseraceae are present everywhere in the world, except in arctic regions. There are six genera. Of the four principal genera, *Aldrovanda*, *Dionaea*, and *Drosophyllum* are each represented by one species only, but the *Drosera* contain a hundred or so species. As the distribution map of the Droseraceae shows, the *Drosera* are ubiquitous, that is they can

be found on all continents; but the genus is best represented in Australia, with 54 species.

Along with their wide geographical distribution there is also a wide morphological diversity of the species. The smallest, pygmy varieties generally grow to no more than ½in (1cm) in height or diameter. Some rampant forms, on the other hand, can reach 3ft (1m) in length. The conditions in which *Drosera*

Drosera adelae, one of the numerous species of the *Drosera* genus. Insects are stuck to the glandular hairs situated on the leaves; × 1.9.

grow (and therefore their cultural requirements) are also very varied. There are species from temperate and tropical climates and others, in the form of tubers, able to endure long periods of drought.

Lentibulariaceae

The Lentibulariaceae are herbaceous plants from damp or boggy soils, or even aquatic conditions. The leaves may be set in different ways or be of various shapes; equally, the traps differ widely between genera. The flowers are hermaphrodite, irregular, solitary or in bunches; they have bilabial corollas, prolonged by a spur, and two stamens. They flower in spring

World distribution of Droseraceae

, *Aldrovanda*

, *Dionaea*

. *Drosophyllum*

. *Drosera*

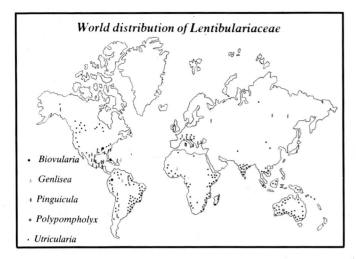

World distribution of Lentibulariaceae

- • Biovularia
- ▴ Genlisea
- ▪ Pinguicula
- ∗ Polypompholyx
- · Utricularia

into compact buds, while those from warmer regions remain in leaf throughout the year. Aquatic species live in calm, acidic waters; terrestrial varieties grow in damp or even boggy soils; and epiphytes develop in tree moss.

Nepenthaceae

The Nepenthaceae are a family of carnivorous plants represented by the single genus *Nepenthes*, which consists of about seventy-two species growing wild. In addition, there are many natural hybrids as well as hybrids created by horticulturists. In their natural state, *Nepenthes* can be found in southeast Asia, Madagascar, and Australia. The islands of Sumatra and Borneo contain the largest number of species, particularly endemic, or truly native ones.

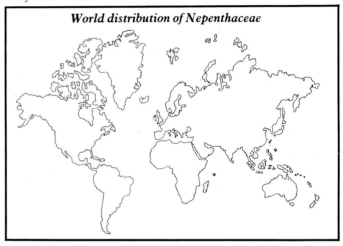

World distribution of Nepenthaceae

or summer. The fruit, resembling a globular or egg-shaped capsule, contains many seeds without albumen.

The Lentibulariaceae family comprises five genera of carnivorous plants. *Biovularia* and *Polypompholyx* each comprise two species. *Biovularia* originate from America; they are small aquatic plants, very similar to species of the closely related genus *Utricularia*, and particularly to *U. vulgaris* and *U. purpurea*. The *Polypompholyx*, of Australian origin, are related to the terrestrial *Utricularia*, from which they can be distinguished by their slightly different utricles, or bladder traps. Today, experts consider that the *Biovularia* and the *Polypompholyx* may both be classified under the genus *Utricularia*.

The *Genlisea*, sixteen species native to Africa, Madagascar, South America, and the West Indies, are very rare in cultivation. They are small aquatic plants that grow half-submerged but with their flowers above the surface. Their traps, which Darwin called 'eel traps', are rather unusual (see page 21).

The species of Lentibulariaceae that are successfully cultivated belong to the *Pinguicula* and *Utricularia* genera. There are more than fifty species of *Pinguicula*; most are natives of the northern hemisphere (America, Europe, Asia) and only five originate from South America. The *Pinguicula* are, in general, terrestrial plants from damp places. They are in the form of a very short, vertical stem surrounded by radical leaves (i.e., growing directly from the roots and lying close to the ground) that form a rosette. The surface of the leaves is shiny, greasy, or sticky, because of the mucus produced by the numerous glands responsible for the capture and digestion of prey; the name *Pinguicula* is in fact derived from the Latin *pinguis*, meaning fat. The leaves give off a mushroom-like smell that attracts insects. According to the species, they are more or less capable of folding in on themselves when an insect touches them, a procedure which increases the amount of contact with the prey. Each stalk bears only one, relatively large flower.

The 275 species of *Utricularia* are either aquatic, terrestrial, or epiphytic. They are found on all continents. The *Utricularia* are plants consisting of stems of lengths up to 10ft (3m) ending in the shape of a strap; the traps, or bladders, are connected to them by a short strand. Cold-climate varieties turn in winter

The name *Nepenthes* is derived (as is the family name) from the Greek word *nêpenthês*, meaning that which dispels sorrow. They are plants with a ligneous stem varying from 8in (20cm) to 65ft (20m) in length and from ¹⁄₁₀in (3mm) to 1¼in (30mm) in diameter. The stem is cylindrical or triangular in section and has two membranous, longitudinal extensions or wings. The plant may climb trees, spread along the ground, or grow short and erect. The leaves are equally variable from one species to another; they are sessile or petiolate. On leaves growing above ground level the central vein, strong and prominent, extends beyond the leaf and forms an appendage as long or even longer than the leaf itself. The tail can twist and serves as an attachment point both for the trap, called an urn, which develops at its extremity, and for the plant as a whole. The urns are of differing shape and allow the various species to be identified; they differ according to their position even within a single species – spherical and often very colourful at the base of the plants, they lengthen and become more cylindrical nearer the top. The urn is topped by an operculum or lid, held in place by a sort of fixed hinge, forming an opening towards the front. The operculum acts as an umbrella, keeping excess water from the trap. Its underside is provided with nectar glands that attract insects. The branched inflorescence of stalked flowers grows directly from the stem at the base of the leaves. The flowers, in simple or composite formation, are many and small. They are brown or greenish in colour, bear no petals, and have a strong, fetid smell.

World distribution of species of Nepenthes		
Country	Total number of species	Number of endemic species
Borneo	30	21
Sumatra	21	11
Malaysia	11	3
Philippines	10	7
New Guinea	10	5
Celebes	6	2
Vietnam	5	4
Moluccas	3	
Java	2	
Madagascar	2	2
Australia	1	
Sri Lanka	1	1
China	1	
India	1	1
New Caledonia	1	
Seychelles	1	1
Palawan	1	

Prolongation of the medial tendril of a *Nepenthes* twisting around a support. At the end of the tendril the trap is beginning to form; × 0.7.

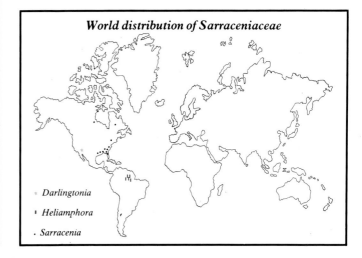

World distribution of Sarraceniaceae

· Darlingtonia
¹ Heliamphora
. Sarracenia

Sarraceniaceae

The Sarraceniaceae are natives of America, where they grow in damp conditions. The flowers appear in spring at the start of the growing period. The long, trumpet-shaped traps are passive. This family comprises three genera. The genus *Darlingtonia* comprises only one species, *D. californica*. The genus *Heliamphora* (from *helios*, sun, and *amphora*, urn) consists of a few high-altitude species, growing naturally in the mountains between the Orinoco and the Amazon in South America. The leaves are folded into a kind of elongated funnel to form the traps. These, varying in size according to the species, measure from 2in (5cm) to 14in (35cm) in height. The stalks are decorated with several flowers, usually white or pale pink, without petals and inclined downwards.

The *Sarracenia* genus has given its name to the family to which it belongs. This name derives from the Quebec doctor M.S. Sarrasin, to whom the first species was dedicated. They are peat-bog plants from North America. They develop from an underground rhizome, from which one or more heads appear, giving rise to leaves in rosette formation. As with the *Heliamphora*, these leaves are folded in, in the shape of a trumpet; they are also topped by an open operculum, the whole

forming the trap or pitcher. According to the species, this can be between 2in (5cm) and 3ft (1m) in height. The stalk bears only one flower, which appears in spring, with five wide, hanging petals, at the base of which are nectar glands. A noticeable and typical feature is the pistil, in the shape of an umbrella turned inside-out.

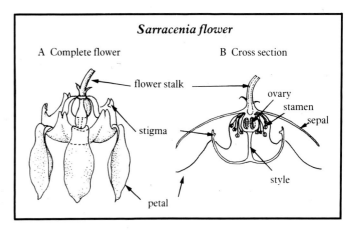

Sarracenia flower

A Complete flower   B Cross section

flower stalk
ovary
stamen
sepal
stigma
style
petal

Capture and absorption of prey

Evolution

As we have seen earlier, carnivorous plants attract, capture, and digest animal prey. These abilities are the result of many millions of years of evolution.

Some carnivorous plants probably derive from plants whose leaves had simple depressions where rainwater could stagnate. Mixed with the decomposing corpses of drowned insects, this water constituted a nutritional medium that the plant could assimilate via its leaves. Such a mechanism can be seen at work in plants alive today – for example, epiphytic *Tillandsia* and, specifically, *Tillandsia usneoides*, which has no roots.

During the course of evolution, the leaves became specialized, with the depressions turning into true pockets whose inner surface gradually acquired nectar-secreting glands to attract insects, and absorption glands, producing mucilage, to dissolve their prey. This outline fits the evolution of those of today's carnivorous plants that have traps like receptacles, where prey is imprisoned.

Plants with sticky tentacles that are capable of attracting and capturing insects descend from plants that made use of hairs covered in a viscous liquid as a means of defence against possible aggressors. They elaborated more and more refined

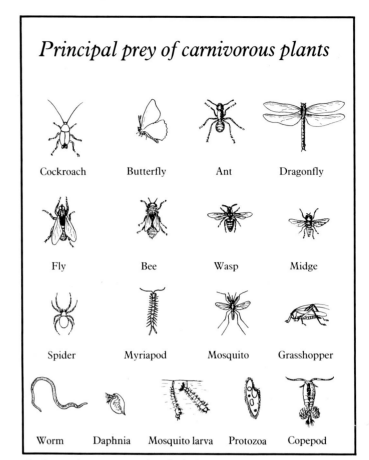

Principal prey of carnivorous plants

Cockroach	Butterfly	Ant	Dragonfly
Fly	Bee	Wasp	Midge
Spider	Myriapod	Mosquito	Grasshopper

Worm   Daphnia   Mosquito larva   Protozoa   Copepod

Carnivorous plants capture a variety of animals.

In the *Pinguicula* (here *Pinguicula vulgaria*), the mucus on the surface of the leaves holds the insects; × 0.5.

Urn-shaped trap of *Nepenthes ventricosa*.
A cockroach larva has been captured; × 1.3.

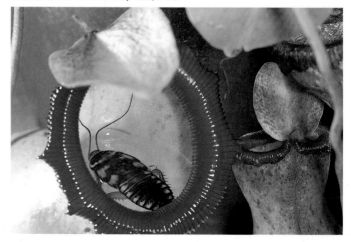

versions of lures and traps, some of which, little by little, acquired movement. Digestive glands also appeared.

Operation of traps

The carnivorous process can be divided into three successive phases – attraction, capture, and digestion. The traps are responsible for both the capture and the digestion of prey.

Attraction

The first stage consists in luring the prey into the trap by some form of deceit. Different methods are used according to the species – odour emission, nectar production, displays of brilliant colours, droplets of mucilage to break up the sunlight into the colours of a spectrum, and so on. Some species use several different strategies simultaneously.

The simplest, and perhaps most effective, lure is the vividly coloured trap, used especially in the *Darlingtonia* and *Nepenthes* species. Colours that stand out from the rest of the plant and the surrounding vegetation never fail to attract insects.

The *Drosera* lure their prey by using small tentacles, the ends of which bear a drop of shiny, glutinous liquid. This equipment serves both to attract and to retain the victims. In the *Byblis*, large numbers of glandular, mucilage-covered hairs decorate all parts of the plant, from the stems to the flower sepals. In its natural habitat and against the sun, this multitude of shining dots is such that the light is broken up as in a rainbow.

The glandular hairs of the *Drosophyllum* produce a mucilage smelling like honey, a substance much appreciated by insects, while those of the *Pinguicula* smell rather like mushrooms. The Venus flytrap is equipped with nectar-secreting glands that attract insects towards the trap. Nectar glands also exist in the genera *Cephalotus*, *Darlingtonia*, *Heliamphora*, *Nepenthes*, and *Sarracenia*.

Capture

Capture constitutes the most spectacular phase of the carnivorous process. The traps used can be categorized according to genus and to the method employed.

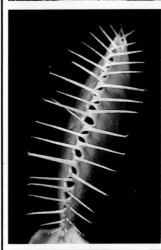 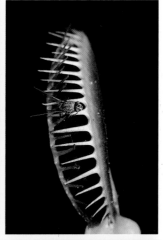

Top: the jaws of a Venus flytrap.
Centre, left: trap having just closed on a victim.
Centre, right: after capture, the trap opens slowly.
Bottom: the two lobes of the trap are completely open: the insect has been digested.

The different types of trap

There are two main categories of trap. Active traps have the power of movement. Passive traps are immobile.

ACTIVE
mousetraps

Mousetraps These traps, which can function only in water, are small bladders, virtually transparent, having at one end an orifice surrounded by outward-branching hairs. These hairs trigger the trap when the prey, which may be microscopic, brushes against them. The bladder then inflates very rapidly, in $1/500$s, drawing in both water and prey. It regains its initial shape in about 30 minutes. Species of the genus *Utricularia* are armed with such traps.

ACTIVE
steel traps

Steel traps The *Dionaea* and *Aldrovanda* species have traps formed from two lobes that close on a central axis like jaws : the outside edges of these lobes are equipped with numerous teeth (from fifteen to twenty in *Dionaea*), which interlock upon closure. This happens the moment a prey makes contact with the sensory hairs. Both lobes, which are slightly concave in the Venus flytrap, then close up and the prey is digested by glands sited on their inner surfaces. Closure can take place in $1/30$s in the *Dionaea* and in $1/500$ to $1/1000$s in *Aldrovanda*.

ACTIVE
fly-paper traps

In *Drosera*, the leaves and tentacles bend inwards at the point where capture is taking place in order to surround the prey with the largest possible number of tentacles. These curve round the victim and direct it towards the digestive glands situated at the cente of the leaves. The whole process can last anything from a minute to a few hours. One or two weeks are required for the tentacles to resume their initial shape.

In *Pinguicula*, the leaves, according to the species, may or may not fold or roll over slightly in order to retain the prey. The tentacles however, smaller and more numerous than in *Drosera*, have no movement at all.

Principles of trap operation Experts have for long inquired into the physiological mechanisms that allow active traps to move in response to external stimuli. The Venus flytrap is probably the most studied species. The transmission of the signal between the hairs stimulated by a prey and the closure mechanism itself probably depends upon differences in electrical potential in the cells beneath the hairs. The electrical signal is passed from cell to cell until it reaches the cells responsible for closure. In the Venus flytrap closure is triggered when one of the sensory hairs is touched twice or when two hairs of the same leaf are touched. It is assumed that this double-trigger action is a safety measure against false alarms, thus avoiding unnecessary closures initiated perhaps by dust or plant debris.

The movement itself is the result of differing growth rates. The trap closes as the result of a sudden growth of cells on the outer surface of the lobes; cells on the inner surface do not grow. This mechanism is reversed when the plant opens.

Digestion

The digestive phase is of varying duration. The digestive glands of *Drosophyllum* can digest a mosquito in one day, while *Utricularia* assimilates its prey a few days after capture.

The general digestive mechanism is similar to that in animals, with the prey finally being transformed into an easily assimilated form. Most species of carnivorous plants are equipped with digestive glands secreting enzymes. Some, however, such as *Heliamphora* and *Darlingtonia*, have no such glands. The prey is decomposed by bacteria present in the liquid in which it drowns and the plant gradually assimilates the nutritive solution thus formed. In *Darlingtonia* the plant adjusts the volume of liquid in the trap to the number of insects

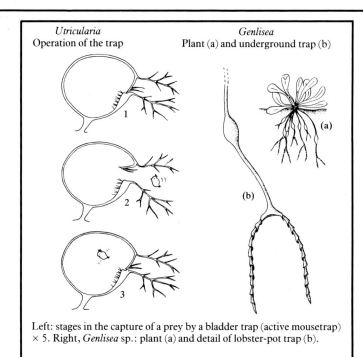

Utricularia
Operation of the trap

Genlisea
Plant (a) and underground trap (b)

Left: stages in the capture of a prey by a bladder trap (active mousetrap) × 5. Right, *Genlisea* sp.: plant (a) and detail of lobster-pot trap (b).

PASSIVE
fly-paper traps

Byblis and *Drosophyllum* have traps armed with glandular hairs, covered with mucilage. These hairs are immobile.

PASSIVE
lobster-pot trap

Nepenthes and *Cephalotus* have leaves ending in urns or pitchers (trumpets surmounted by a cover called an operculum). Prey, attracted by nectar glands, enter the trap and slip on the internal walls, which are topped by an impassable, rolled edge; they end up drowning, as in the trumpet traps.

PASSIVE
pitfall traps

Sarracenia, *Darlingtonia*, and *Heliamphora* have pitfall traps made from leaves in the shape of trumpets. Insects, attracted by nectar glands, enter through the opening, situated near the top of the trap. Its inner wall is slippery or covered with hairs pointing downwards, preventing any retreat. Victims drown in the liquid at the bottom of the trap.

The *Genlisea* have a very special trap, which Darwin nicknamed the 'eel trap'. It consists of an egg-shaped, hollow bulb, lengthening into a sort of cylindrical tube which has at its very end a slit opening; this is elongated into two arms and is shaped like a fork. Victims entering the orifice are firmly held by small hairs. They are gradually drawn towards the bulb, which acts as a sort of stomach.

captured. *Nepenthes* have a dual action – they use both bacteria and enzymes.

Traps of this sort are very successful, but some insects have found ways of defeating them. In the urns of *Nepenthes masoalensis*, a Madagascan species, one often finds, besides the remains of captured insects, aquatic larvae of various insects and, especially, of mosquitos alive and well in the solution. This can only mean that certain insects have adapted to outwit the traps laid for them by carnivorous plants.

Digestive glands and sensory hair inside a Venus flytrap; × 36.

General principles of cultivation

A fine specimen of *Nepenthes* × *chelsonii* growing in a hanging basket in a well-lit position; × 0.3.

A 'natural' environment created in a garden or greenhouse is ideal for cultivating carnivorous plants. If you have only a terrace or apartment it is still possible to cultivate a variety of species. The following paragraphs give the general principles of cultivation.

Composts and cultivation media

Carnivorous plants can be subdivided into four categories:
   plants from relatively dry climates;
   plants from damp or boggy sites;
   tropical plants, *Nepenthes* type;
   aquatic plants.

Dry climate plants

Only the genus *Drosophyllum* enters into this category and for this see page 90.

Damp or boggy site plants

Compost These plants grow on acid soil and sphagnum moss is the best growing medium to use because of its ability to bring down the pH to 5, even if the water used has a higher pH level.

Sphagnum is a moss from swampy grounds and there are a number of varieties. Large-headed moss should be chosen because it is more durable and of better quality than other sorts. Sphagnum has the advantage of being very hygroscopic – in other words it retains a lot of water, so much so that it can absorb a quantity of water equivalent to ten times its own dry weight.

This capacity of sphagnum to retain water allows it to be used to supply a slatted propagation bench, placed between 2-12in (5-30cm) above a large tray of water. The water is transmitted to the bench by capillary action by means of a few tufts of sphagnum placed 'chimney fashion' between the bench and the water. The water thus conveyed is purified in its passage through the moss.

The disadvantage of sphagnum moss is that it establishes itself and grows into the pots until it overruns the smaller plants. Therefore it must be trimmed or the 'heads' pricked off. These can then be used for replanting. When raising seedlings or very small plants, the sphagnum can be sterilized in boiling water, but two weeks must be allowed to pass before using it, in order to avoid the development of fungi. A healthy sphagnum moss is the sign of good propagation and means that the water is of good quality.

If sphagnum is not available, the next best compost is peat. Peat, too, can raise the pH of the water to 5. It is better to choose sphagnum-based peat and not to use the 'enriched' types which contain feed. A fibrous quality is preferable to a powdery one.

Other composts may be used for the propagation of carnivorous plants. They must, though, be porous and contain few salts and nutritional matter. Sand is a possibility. Quarry sand and beach sand are not recommended. River sand is best, but it should be thoroughly washed before use no matter how clean the site from which it came.

One compost mixture used quite frequently is that made up of half river sand and half non-enriched peat. This should be thoroughly mixed and well watered, then allowed to stand for two weeks before use so that microflora can grow and sufficient acidity can be produced. Perlite, a natural silicate in particle form, may be introduced. The mixture then, prepared in the same way, is one-third sand, one-third peat, and one-third fine perlite.

Fertilizer In theory, carnivorous plants ought to find enough nourishment in the mixtures mentioned above, provided that they catch insects. But when there are few or no insects, particularly indoors, some experts recommend the use of very dilute fertilizers, either in the form of a foliar spray or introduced into the urns. Balanced feeds should be used in doses not exceeding a tenth of those recommended for normal use with indoor plants. Monthly application during the growing period is sufficient.

The appearance of algae on the edges of pots is almost always a sign of excess phosphate. Sphagnum is still the best indicator of good propagation: withering is a sign of too much feed or of poor quality water.

Sphagnum moss, used here for the propagation of *Drosera filiformis*, is a suitable compost for plants that are not too small.

Tropical plants – the *Nepenthes*

Species of the genus *Nepenthes* are often epiphytic in their natural state. Hanging baskets placed near the greenhouse glass are ideal, but perforated pots in terracotta or plastic can also be used to obtain beautiful plants bearing many urns.

They are plants that feed mainly on humus. The compost must be porous and well drained. Sphagnum is the only ideal medium, but growers sometimes show extraordinary examples cultivated in a variety of soils (see table below).

In fact any of these composts can be used for propagating *Nepenthes*, but certain rules must be followed according to which one is chosen. Plants growing in orchid composts require watering fortnightly and feeding during the growing

---

Compost mixtures for propagating Nepenthes

1 ½ sphagnum
  ½ pine bark
2 ½ sphagnum
  ½ orchid compost (see mixture no. 9)
3 ⅓ sphagnum moss
  ⅓ polypodium roots (*Polypodium vulgare*)
  ⅓ heath mould (fragmented, not reduced to powder) or leaf mould
  Polypodium is a fern whose fine fibres have long been used in the cultivation of orchids.
4 ⅓ polypodium
  ⅓ sphagnum
  ⅓ beech or oak leaf mould
5 ½ polypodium
  ½ sphagnum
6 Cultivation in pure, fibrous peat. Ordinary peats are too compacted and insufficiently aerated.
7 ⅕ sphagnum
  ⅕ fibrous peat
  ⅕ pine bark
  ⅕ perlite
  ⅕ decomposed manure
8 ⅕ sphagnum
  ⅕ polypodium
  ⅕ leaf mould
  ⅕ perlite
  ⅕ decomposed manure
9 Normal mixtures for orchid composts, with a base of pine bark; eg:

Mixture 1
⁷⁄₁₀ pine bark
²⁄₁₀ expanded clay
¹⁄₁₀ polyurethane foam

Mixture 2
⁵⁄₁₀ pine bark
²⁄₁₀ fibrous peat
¹⁄₁₀ polyurethane
¹⁄₁₀ perlite
¹⁄₁₀ polystyrene

period. From March to September the compost must be kept very damp, without ever allowing it to dry out. In winter, the plants should be watered much more sparingly. At all times rainwater only should be used.

Liquid feeds can be used in quantities equal to half those recommended by the makers, when the compost contains no sphagnum; when it does, an amount ten times less than that recommended must not be exceeded or the sphagnum may die, putting at risk the whole operation. Feeds are usually available in balanced formulae or in organic form.

Crushed charcoal can be added to all mixtures for *Nepenthes* since it decontaminates the compost; however, the total quantity must not exceed $\frac{1}{20}$ of the whole.

Aquatic plants

The cultivation of aquatic carnivorous plants involves the use of pure and acid water. For safety, it is advisable to check the acidity of the water from time to time using a pH meter. There are two kinds: colour-coded meters, which are excellent value, and those with a scale – battery or mains operated. The pH level must never be below 4 nor more than 6. The ideal degree of acidity is between 4.5 and 5.5. Such an acidity is not always easy to maintain. For example, the pH of rainwater collected in a cement container is 7, which is not very suitable. One method

Utricularia inflata, an aquatic species. Cultivation of this type of plant necessitates careful control of the chemical composition of the water.

of lowering the pH is to coat the inside of the container with a special waterproof paint or with a film of plastic.

Whatever kind of container is used, the water can also be acidified by placing a layer of peat in the bottom of the basin. The peat must be soaked in water beforehand, or it will tend to float. Sphagnum can replace peat or be added to it, since it has the same properties. Water of a precisely determined acidity can also be obtained chemically, by adding to it, in order of preference, phosphoric acid, nitric acid, or sulphuric acid. These acids are dangerous to use and must not be allowed to come into contact with the skin. When the container is small, the acid must be added drop by drop with a pipette. It is best to stir continually during this procedure and to check the pH level frequently. If, on the other hand, the water is too acid and it is to be made more alkaline (i.e., its pH value raised), one only needs to add limestone powder (calcium), ammonia, potash, or even soda, regularly checking the rise in pH.

Potting and re-potting

Materials and equipment

Type of pot Containers are on sale in shops in many forms and a choice has to be made. Plastic pots are more and more widespread but terracotta pots can still be found. The clay pot is quite useful because of its porosity and thus its ability to retain water, but it is no longer being much used in cultivation because its inner walls absorb accumulated salts, which gradually harm the plants. This is why clay pots should only be used new. Plastic pots have the advantage, among others, of being easy to clean. The water must be constantly renewed and so plastic pots without drainage holes must not be used or there is a risk of stagnant water accumulating.

Size of pot The importance of choosing a pot of the right diameter cannot be over-emphasized. If there is a choice between two sizes, take the smaller. If the plant eventually outgrows its pot, it can be taken out along with its root ball, without exposing the roots, and placed in a larger container, packing compost all round. To remove the plant, complete with root ball, simply invert the pot, placing the fingers of one hand on the compost on both sides of the plant to keep it in place; holding the pot with the other hand, tap its edge against a hard object, such as a table edge, in order to loosen the root ball.

Potting

Position of the plant in the pot An important point in repotting is the height at which the plant should be in the compost. If, for example, one is potting a species of the genus *Sarracenia* or of the genus *Darlingtonia*, the pitchers must not be in the soil and their bases should remain above the compost, but the rhizome must not be visible. In species of other genera, the parts that should be in the soil are easily distinguishable from those that should be above the ground. With the Venus flytrap, for example, all the leaves should sit above the compost.

The plant must occupy the centre of the pot if it has a rosette of leaves. Rhizome plants of the genus *Sarracenia* or *Darlingtonia* are positioned so that they have enough room to develop new growth; old pitchers that have stopped growing may be placed against the edges of the pot. If the plant has a tuft-like appearance, showing that it is liable to grow many new shoots in all directions, the pot must be large enough to allow for this.

Packing The compost must not be too compacted; in order to retain its properties, it must be only lightly packed so that when it dries air may replace the water and so that roots may easily penetrate it.

Nepenthes – a special case

Repotting of *Nepenthes* takes place from January on – in spring at the latest. All decomposed matter must be cleared from the roots. Soak the root ball in a bucket of water, shake the plant, and the old compost will disintegrate. The plant can then be potted in fresh compost.

Nepenthes often grows vigorously and it is best to support the stems of the faster-growing species and hybrids. *Nepenthes* must be trimmed frequently in order to obtain the best urns. Trimming the upper part of the plant encourages shoots to form at the base; these are in turn trimmed as soon as they are sufficiently high. In this way, lovely plants can be grown, having a good number of well-spaced urns from the base upwards. The top of the plant, trimmed at each stage, can be used for cuttings.

Ambient conditions

Humidity

Most carnivorous plants come from sites that are perpetually damp. This dampness is not only in the soil but also comes from the evaporation of surrounding water and can, when the temperature reaches a certain level, raise the humidity to saturation point. It is not possible to reproduce such conditions in a greenhouse, still less in an apartment.

Miniature greenhouses are able to conserve humidity but at the same time there is insufficient renewal of air and, if the plants are exposed to the sun, they may be scorched. Larger greenhouses can have more sophisticated equipment and their 'climates' set automatically. Plants placed outdoors, in the garden or on the balcony, need a good, nightly watering.

A fine specimen of *Sarracenia rubra*, propagated in a plastic pot. The compost contains fresh sphagnum; × 0.3.

Benches filled with gravel and water also maintain some humidity. Humidifiers are an ideal means of supplementing this supply of moisture.

Light

The best source of light is the sun and many carnivorous species benefit from full sunlight, which has the effect of hardening the plant and, in genera such as *Dionaea*, *Sarracenia*, and *Drosera*, of bringing out the brightest colours.

Nonetheless, plants can be grown successfully under artificial light if daylight, white light, or grow-lux fluorescent tubes are used. These are specially designed for plant cultivation, but they are rather expensive. Incandescent lamps, floodlights, and spotlights have a tendency to overheat the interior of small greenhouses. They also use a large amount of electricity.

Semi-immersion watering means keeping the bases of pots in a tray with sides 4in (10cm) high. There should always be ½-1in (1-2cm) of water at the bottom.

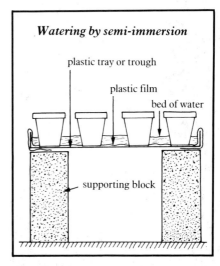

Watering by semi-immersion

plastic tray or trough

plastic film

bed of water

supporting block

Most carnivorous plants cultivated under tubes or bulbs need plenty of light. Lamps need to be placed about 12in (30cm) above the plants. Ideally, fluorescent tubes should be grouped in twos or fours and mounted in suitable reflectors. Tall plants also need lateral lighting.

The advantage of artificial lighting is that it allows not only the duration of light to be regulated by means of a timer, but also the intensity to be controlled by varying the distance of the plant from the light source – the intensity of the light is in inverse proportion to the distance. For guidance, the following examples may be given: cultivation in full sun corresponds to an illumination of 40,000 to 80,000lx (lx being the symbol for lux, the unit of light); to obtain its equivalent in artificial light, 5,000 to 20,000lx are needed for fourteen to sixteen hours per day; cultivation in shade represents 10,000 to 30,000lx, which, in artificial light, requires a minimum of 1,000 to 10,000lx for fourteen to sixteen hours per day.

It is estimated that an indoor plant, in a window facing north, receives 2,200 to 5,000lx of natural light 12in (30cm) from the window and 1,000 to 1,900lx at a distance of 3ft (1m). A 75W incandescent light bulb gives 1,600lx at a distance of 12in (30cm) and 410lx at 3ft (1m), while an

An example of shelving allowing the cultivation of carnivorous plants inside an apartment or house. Light is supplied by fluorescent tubes.

A large greenhouse for propagating carnivorous plants, containing mainly *Sarracenia*. Venus flytraps can also be seen. The greenhouse roof has been drawn back so that the plants can have the benefit of direct sunlight and acquire vivid colours. Netting prevents birds from pecking in the compost.

ordinary 100W electric lamp produces 430lx at the same distance. Finally, a fluorescent tube of 40W gives 1,290lx at 12in (30cm) and 800lx at 2ft (60cm).

Temperature

In the growing period, temperatures must not exceed 30°-37°C during the day. The minimum at night must not go below 5°C.

Nepenthes – Special conditions

For the cultivation of species of the genus *Nepenthes* there are extra details to be observed in addition to the preceding general points. Being native to damp, tropical regions, these plants must be cultivated in a very humid atmosphere – orchid greenhouses are perfect for them. If a greenhouse is not available, the plants can be placed above trays filled with gravel and water or, better still, humidifiers can be used. In any case, the relative humidity must not be below 70 per cent.

Species of the genus *Nepenthes* living in full sunlight in their natural habitat are quite rare and the average luminosity to be observed in propagation must correspond to 50 per cent sunlight – i.e., 'half shade'. The temperature can vary from a minimum of 15°C to a maximum of 35°C. Minimum temperatures of around 5-10°C are bearable by high-altitude species, which must be kept in a cool greenhouse.

Rest

Rest is important during cultivation. Rest is to plants what sleep is to animals. Instead of a daily sleep, plants have a rest period corresponding to winter (or very rarely to the dry season). If plants are cultivated without regard to this rest period they will eventually degenerate and die. The characteristics of this resting stage vary according to species and their origins. *Pinguicula vulgaris* is a species that, when fixed to a damp rock, can withstand temperatures of 30°C in summer and of −20°C in winter, while *Pinguicula caudata* dies below 0°C. But both, like all carnivorous plants, must experience every year a definite seasonal change and pass through a stage of winter recovery, with short days, less light, cooler temperatures, and lower humidity.

During the rest period, watering must be reduced, although the compost must still be kept slightly damp. In artificial lighting, the number of hours of light should be less and the lamps moved further away so as to imitate natural conditions.

Terrarium

A terrarium is an interior greenhouse that allows automatic control of humidity, temperature, and light. Certain manufacturers design terraria to suit the locality in which they will be used and the plants they will contain. Ventilation is necessary in order to avoid condensation on the glass – a sign of a stuffy atmosphere in which the plants will wilt and parasitic fungus will be encouraged. Artificial light allows the terrarium to be placed on the northern side of an apartment. If it is exposed to full sunlight, suitable shade will be required. The terrarium could, if wished, be placed in a larger greenhouse to form a separate section with different conditions of cultivation. A terrarium's main advantage is that it conserves humidity, so that fewer waterings are needed. Also, the automatic regulation of temperature and light intensity provides ideal conditions in which to keep one's favourite plants close by. In order to avoid the water stagnating, cultivation trays with a slatted base are necessary: the water rises by capillary action from a container placed underneath. Cultivation requirements differ from one genus to another, even sometimes from one species to another, particularly concerning the period of rest. That is why it is recommended to keep potted plants buried in peat or sphagnum with the upper part still visible: in this way the humidity can be controlled. The following genera can be cultivated in a terrarium: *Aldrovanda*, *Byblis*, *Cephalotus*, *Drosera*, *Utricularia*, *Heliamphora*, *Pinguicula*, *Sarracenia*, and *Darlingtonia*.

Pests and diseases

Carnivorous plants have their enemies, which may be fungi or animals, principally insects (aphids, mealy bugs, scale insects, thrips, whiteflies, ants, butterfly larvae) and red spiders, wood lice, slugs, snails, small mammals, and birds.

Generally speaking, precautions must be taken to limit the risk of attack: leaves or any other part of the plant, dead or dying, must be removed and the affected plant cleaned. If a leaf or flower becomes mildewed, this can develop into large-scale decay. In cases where a plant is attacked by an insect or where it is diseased, it must be quarantined for as long as it remains untreated, in order to avoid any further contamination. Finally, one must ensure good ventilation. Apart from these principles, there are specific treatments for each type of pest or disease.

A pitcher of a cobra lily (*Darlingtonia californica*) attacked by the *Oïdium* fungus; × 1.5.

Fungi

Fungi may belong to either the *Botrytis* or the *Oïdium* genus. Their structure is that of a thallus – i.e. composed of filaments of cells and having no leaves, roots, or chlorophyll. Fungus development normally begins with the formation of white blotches, which rapidly increase in size. The affected plants turn grey or black and their chlorophyll disappears. These attacks are the result of a rise in temperature and a lack of light; plants cultivated in open sunlight are not affected.

Treatment
The affected parts must be cut away at the start of the infestation. The plants must be isolated and their containers not re-used. In addition they may be sprayed with, or soaked in, a fungicide.

Aphids at different stages of
development; × 8.

Large numbers of red aphids
on a stalk; × 8.

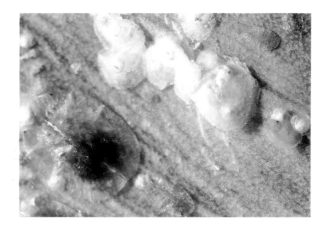

Scale insects, in the form of small cushions,
at different stages of development; × 12.

Aphids

Aphids are large enough to be visible to the naked eye. They may or may not be winged but if they are the upper wings are larger than the lower ones. The body is globular, oval, and soft. At the rear of the abdomen are two hollow stalks from which a sugary substance is excreted and used to feed the young; this substance attracts ants, for whom this is a delicacy. The head bears two antennae, slightly longer than half the body. A curved beak or proboscis allows aphids to suck plant sap for their food. Their legs are long and thin. Their presence is detectable by a malformation of the affected parts of the plant, by a sticky black deposit, or by the white bodies of dead insects at the base of the plant.

The colour of the insects varies: they might be yellow, black, or green; they are partly camouflaged on leaves.

Treatment
Several proprietary insecticides will kill aphids, but they must be used with care. Always follow the manufacturer's instructions. Fumigation can be used if the greenhouse is not attached to the dwelling; before using this method, it is advisable to consult the suppliers of the product.

Mealy bugs and scale insects

Mealy bugs and scale insects are very destructive, but fortunately they rarely occur on carnivorous plants. Most vulnerable are *Darlingtonia*, *Nepenthes*, and *Sarracenia*. The insects suck plant sap and inject substances that discolour the affected tissue and cause its decay. They can also transmit certain viral infections.

Mealy bugs Soft and mobile, these are white with a ringed body, oval shaped, and ¼in (6mm) long in the adult state; their bodies often end in two very long appendices.

Scale insects These come in many colours – white, grey, yellow, brown, mahogany, or red. They form small cushions, which are filled with a large quantity of tiny eggs, on the plants.

Treatment
Treatment is with a suitable proprietary insecticide. Greenhouses situated well away from dwellings may be fumigated, but fumigation is a technique that requires certain precautionary measures; to avoid inhaling toxic fumes carry out the treatment in the evening and ventilate well the following morning. Additionally, cold-blooded animals can be adversely affected, so care must be taken with any insecticide used in fumigation.

Red spiders and other mites

Two types of mite are liable, albeit rarely, to infest carnivorous plants.

Red spider mites These mobile mites are tiny – on average only ¹⁄₅₀in (0.5mm) long. They have six legs as larvae, eight later, and are of variable colour, going from white to yellow and to red. These mites develop on dry plants, since they dislike dampness. They weave fine webs and bite the leaves to suck out the sap; the leaves

Thrips in the larval stage (round the edge) and winged adults (centre); × 23.

Thrips

These are tiny insects with four long, narrow, fringed wings. Yellowish-white in the young stage, in the adult stage they become grey-brown with a black cross on the top of the abdomen. Rarely seen on carnivorous plants, they can nevertheless develop on neighbouring plants. Their presence has been noted on *Nepenthes* in reviews dating back more than a century. They move around freely, attacking above all young leaves which they bite in order to suck out the sap or, in the case of females, to lay their eggs in the tissues.

Treatment
Thrips prefer a dry atmosphere and humidity is normally enough to keep them at bay. Otherwise spray insecticides may be used or, in enclosed greenhouses not attached to dwellings, fumigation products may be preferred.

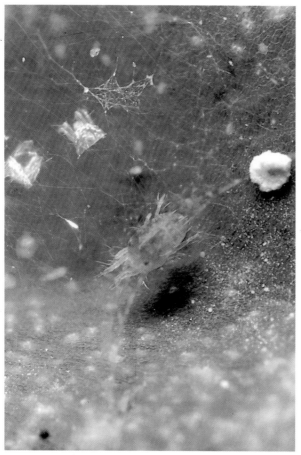

A red spider mite having woven its web; × 40.

then lose their colour, because the bites reduce their cholorophyll content.
Phytoptes Sedentary and usually red in colour, these parasites are capable of destroying plants.

Treatment
The best treatment against these mites is humidity; frequent soaking or misting prevents them from becoming established. However, if they do occur on plants, they can be eliminated by using a proprietary insecticide according to the maker's instructions.

An unwary whitefly caught in the glandular tentacles of a carnivorous plant; × 23.

Whitefly

These are the small, white insects that fly up when the plants are shaken. They feed on plant sap. They attack most carnivorous plants, but only in small numbers.

Treatment

An insectide spray may be used. Treatment should be given every three days for two weeks, since insecticides do not destroy the eggs. Another means of eliminating whitefly is to capitalize on their attraction for the colour yellow: they can be trapped on panels coated with glue.

Caterpillars

Butterflies produce larvae called caterpillars, some of which are particularly attracted to various carnivorous plants, such as the *Pinguicula*. Caterpillars are easy to spot, despite their colour, which is often identical to that of the leaves. As there are usually very few of them, they can simply be lifted off.

A *Pinguicula caudata* eaten by caterpillars, whose droppings can be seen; × 0.4.

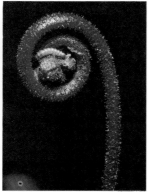

A caterpillar feeding on the flower stalk of a *Drosera neo-caledonica;* × 4.

The small caterpillar of *Papaipema appassionata* penetrates the rhizomes of certain *Sarracenia*. It can be spotted by the piles of droppings left at the base of the plant.

Treatment

Caterpillars on leaves can usually simply be picked off. Those that have penetrated rhizomes can be destroyed by widening the entrance hole before picking them out with laboratory tweezers, but it is not easy. Another method is to introduce an insecticide into the rhizome with a medical needle and syringe.

Other pests

Ants These do not attack plants directly but they can help the spread of aphids, mealy bugs, and scale insects. They are rarely encountered in collections of carnivorous plants, the atmosphere being too humid for them. However, where their presence constitutes a risk, they can be destroyed using a number of preparations sold in different forms (bait, granules, etc).

Wood lice These arthropods are not very dangerous for carnivorous plants; they feed on dead vegetable matter. If there are too many of them, they can be caught using lightly hollowed-out potato halves, under which they will take refuge overnight. They can then be destroyed with an insecticide.

Snails and slugs The presence of these molluscs is betrayed by the tracks they leave behind and by the holes they make in the leaves and flowers. They can be trapped with lettuce leaves put down in the evening and collected and destroyed in the morning. Proprietary slug baits, normally in the form of pellets, are also effective.

House and field mice These rodents can occasionally damage carnivorous plants, usually the Venus flytrap. They are easily eliminated using traps or poisoned bait available in the shops.

Birds Blackbirds especially, during dry spells, rummage in the damp compost to the point where the roots of certain plants become completely exposed. The most effective treatment consists of anti-bird nets.

Choice and cultivation

The choice of your first carnivorous plant depends on the locality or the amount of room available for cultivation, and therefore on the size of your dwelling: apartment, house with a veranda or garden, etc.

Indoor growing

Indoors, it is important to position plants correctly: species that like full sun must, of course, be placed on windowsills facing south. Care must be taken that the temperature does not exceed the limit that each species can tolerate and in particular that it does not go over 35°C behind glass. One of the most interesting and suitable species to grow in this situation is the Venus flytrap. As soon as the weather permits the window should be left open to expose the plant to fresh air and sunlight or, when there is no longer a risk of frost, it can be put outside on the window ledge.

Other species suitable for growing inside a south-facing window include those of the genus *Sarracenia*, particularly *Sarracenia flava*. *Drosera* also grow happily in this position, as long as the special propagation needs of each species are observed. East- or west-facing windows, as long as they are not too exposed, can be used for growing these plants, as well as *Cephalotus follicularis* and the *Utricularia*. North-facing windows only allow *Aldrovanda vesiculosa* and species of *Pinguicula* to be grown. Propagation in a dark apartment is possible, at a pinch, thanks to fluorescent lights or neon tubes of the daylight type. Plants that can be cultivated in artificial light are species of *Drosera*, *Drosophyllum*, *Utricularia*, *Pinguicula*, and *Cephalotus*.

Outdoor growing

If you live in a house with a veranda, this can often provide, through good exposure to the sun, ideal conditions for the cultivation of carnivorous plants. If you have a garden, hardy species can be placed in a peat bog and kept there all year round. To make a peat bog, first dig out the ground to the desired size and shape, then place along the bottom a sheet of thick plastic, hugging the contours of the ground, just as you would prepare for a waterproof basin (see drawing). This small pond can be quite deep if it is to take aquatic plants (*Utricularia* and *Aldrovanda*, for example). Around the edge, water soaks into the peat forming a swamp that becomes less and less wet nearer the outer edge. Plants that can be left all year round in a peat bog are those species of *Drosera* and *Pinguicula* from cold or temperate climates, as well as *Sarracenia flava*, *Sarracenia purpurea* var. *purpurea*, and *Darlingtonia californica*. The Venus flytrap can be kept in peat at temperatures down to −5°C – it will survive, though not thrive. Species of other genera (*Byblis*, *Cephalotus*, and *Heliamphora*) are equally suitable, as long as they are protected from frost during the winter. For species remaining out all winter in the peat bog, frost protection can be ensured by the use of cold frames covered with a sheet of quilted or bubble-wrap plastic or with matting when there is a sharp frost.

In fact, probably only *Nepenthes* are unsuitable for peat-bog cultivation. On the other hand, species of this genus adapt very well to greenhouse cultivation.

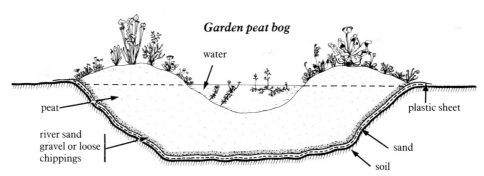

Garden peat bog

water

peat

river sand
gravel or loose
chippings

plastic sheet

sand

soil

The dimensions of a garden peat bog will vary according to the amount of space available, but its depth must be at least 20in (50cm). Stones containing no chalk can be added to improve the appearance.

Traps and Flowers

Dionaea muscipula (Venus flytrap). Active steel trap. The closed traps are in the process of digestion.
They will re-open when the insect has been digested; × 6.5

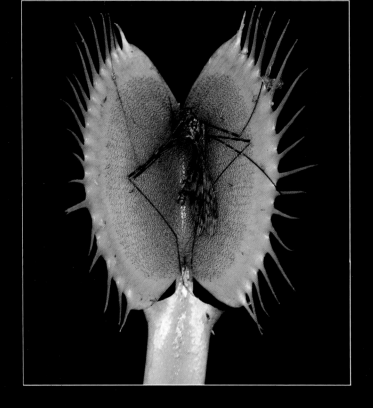

Dionaea muscipula. Active steel trap.
The only parts remaining of this digested
mosquito are the cuticle and the wings.

Utricularia dichotoma. Active mousetrap. Close-up of the bladder or trap, with its trigger hairs ready for prey – in this case tiny earthworms; × 27.

Drosera capensis (Cape Drosera). **Active fly-paper trap. A mosquito is stuck to the tentacles. The leaf limb folds in towards the prey to facilitate capture;** × 7.

Drosera marchantii. Active fly-paper trap. Close-up of a leaf with its long tentacles for capturing prey; × 13.

Drosera auriculata. Active fly-paper trap. The frail-looking stalk that bears the traps grows to 12in (30cm); × 1.7.

Drosera binata. Active fly-paper trap. A butterfly is glued between two 'branches' of a leaf; × 4.

Drosera macrophylla. **Active fly-paper trap. The leaves, in rosette formation, are very large. A few captured midges can be seen, stuck to the surface; × 1.8.**

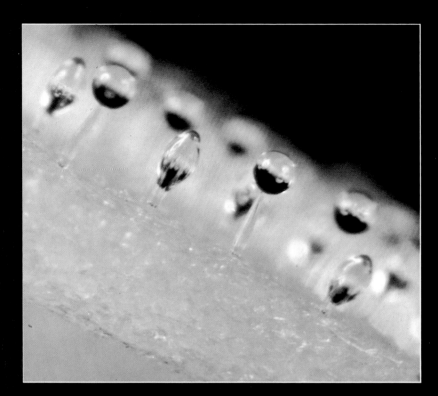

Pinguicula moranensis. **Active fly-paper trap. Greatly enlarged section of a leaf, showing the pendunculate glands ending in a drop of mucilage;** × 60.

Pinguicula moranensis. **Active fly-paper trap. The leaves, which are the capturing part of the plant, spread out over the soil. The flowers raise themselves well clear of them;** × 1.5.

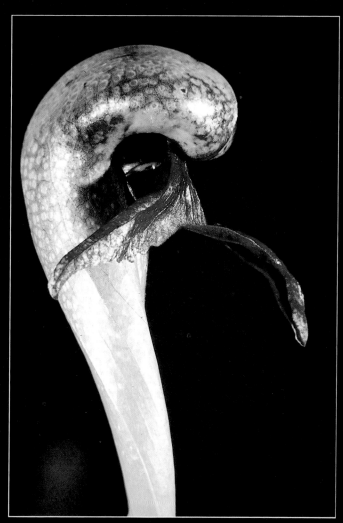

Darlingtonia californica. Passive pitfall trap. The trap entrance is situated under the 'dome'; × 1.5.

Heliamphora minor. Passive pitfall trap. A cockroach larva is about to enter one of the traps; × 1.

Brocchinia reducta. Passive pitfall trap. A species of the Bromeliaceae family, recently considered to be carnivorous; × 1.5.

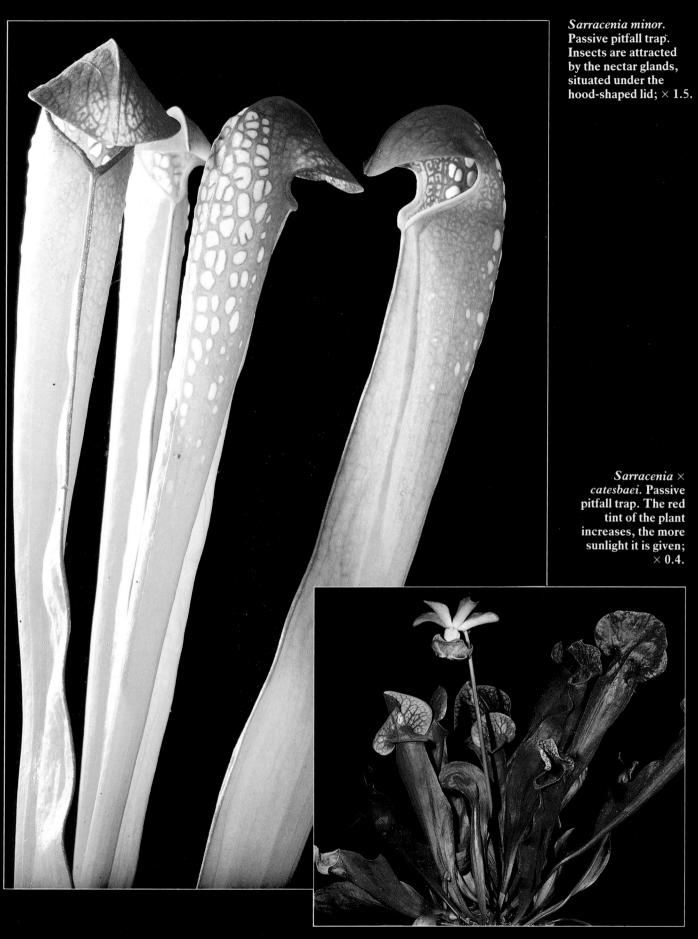

Sarracenia minor.
Passive pitfall trap.
Insects are attracted
by the nectar glands,
situated under the
hood-shaped lid; × 1.5.

Sarracenia ×
catesbaei. Passive
pitfall trap. The red
tint of the plant
increases, the more
sunlight it is given;
× 0.4.

Nepenthes rafflesiana. Passive pitfall trap. Upper part of a trap, surmounted by the lid, armed with a 'spur'; × 4.5.

Nepenthes × ville de rouen. Passive pitfall trap. Trap, supported by the elongation of the leaf blade; × 0.8.

Cephalotus follicularis. (Albany pitcher plant). Passive pitfall trap. Attracted by nectar glands, a cockroach larva enters one of the traps; × 4.

Nepenthes ventricosa. Passive pitfall trap. A wonderfully ornamental plant. Bottom right, a young urn is not yet open; × 0.8.

Nepenthes sanguinea. Passive pitfall trap. The colour of the traps has given it its name; × 0.6.

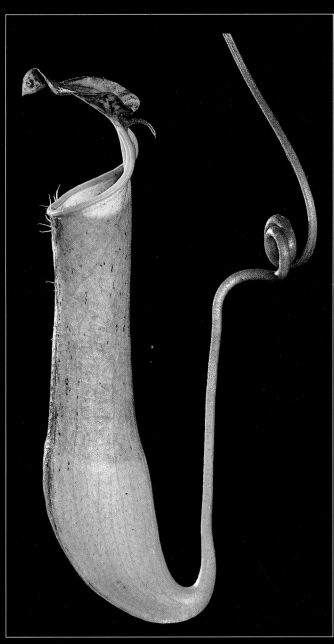

Nepenthes gracilis. Passive pitfall trap. An urn and the 'tendril' that supports it; × 2.5.

Drosera modesta. Flower with the 'hairy' pistil, surrounded by the stamens; × 4.

Drosera capensis. (Cape sundew). The stamens are yellow, the stigmas and petals are pink; × 3.5.

Pinguicula* × *sethos. The colour of the flower is reminiscent of some orchids; × 3.

Drosera macrophylla. The perfumed flower attracts insects, thereby ensuring pollinization; × 3.5.

Pinguicula caerulea and *P. lutea* (from left to right). Flower shape remains constant but the colour varies according to the species; × 4.

Sarracenia purpurea; S. rubra (from top to bottom).
All flowers of Sarracenia have the same typical aspect; × 0.9.

Utricularia alpina. The lower petal, or labellum, is well

Nepenthes kampotiana. Bunch of female flowers; × 4.

Nepenthes sp. Bunch of male flowers; × 4.

Nepenthes 'tendril' ending with a young urn just forming; × 3.

Part Three
PRINCIPAL SPECIES IN CULTIVATION

Dionaea muscipula

Active steel trap

Venus flytrap

Family Droseraceae.
Genus The genus *Dionaea* contains only one species, *D. muscipula*.
Common names Venus flytrap; French, *dionée*; German, *Venus Fliegenfalle*.
Origin North and South Carolina.

	Size	*4-6in (10-15cm) in diameter*
	Exposure	*full sun*
	Cultivation	*in pots*
	Humidity	*constant*
	Temperature	*0° to 37°C*
	Flowers	*early summer*
	Life span	*indefinite*

History and etymology

The Venus flytrap was the first species of carnivorous plant to attract the attention of botanists. Although first mentioned in 1743, it was 'discovered' only around 1760, by Dobbs, governor of North Carolina. Linnaeus, although he classified it among 'sensitive' plants, was not convinced that it was carnivorous. Ellis, who studied the plant, and described it as 'a machine which captures its own food', thought that the prey-detecting hairs were spines intended to pierce the insects. It was left to Charles Darwin eventually to demonstrate the carnivorous nature of the Venus flytrap. Linnaeus bestowed the generic name in recognition of the plant's beauty – the name comes from Diana, Greek goddess and mother of Aphrodite, who is the equivalent of the Roman Venus, goddess of beauty.

Habitat

In its natural state the Venus flytrap can be found in savanna plains, where there are few bushes or trees, in North and South Carolina.

It often grows surrounded by grasses and by other carnivorous plants (species of the genera *Sarracenia*, *Drosera*, *Utricularia*, and *Pinguicula*), on damp soils

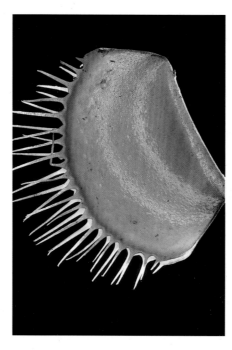

The trap of a Venus flytrap, side view. The teeth on each of the two lobes enmesh; × 1.9.

able to withstand dry spells. The surface of the soil is peaty and the subsoil sandy or loamy, with an acid pH of between 4 and 5. The roots go down on average to 4in (10cm) – a depth that allows the plant to survive bush fires and then to regrow.

High temperatures do not harm plants, which can be cultivated in full sunlight as long as the humidity is sufficiently high. At the other extreme, Venus flytraps withstand light frosts in their original habitats and they have been left in open ground throughout the winter with temperatures going down to about −7°C without any problem. However, plants grown in pots in the open air can perish at −3°C.

Description

Dimension In adult plants the total length of the leaves reaches 2¾in (7cm). The flower stalks are 4-14in (10-35cm) high.
Morphology Four to eight leaves, in rosette formation, grow from a short rhizome, surrounded by the bases of the petioles. Each leaf comprises a wedge-shaped stalk ¾in-2¼in (2-6cm) in length, flat, narrow at the base and at its extremity reaching ¾in (2cm) or more in width; the leaf stalk ends with the two lobes of the trap. These are of variable size according to age and conditions of cultivation – ⅜in-1¼in (1-3cm) long and ³⁄₁₆-¹¹⁄₁₆in (5-17mm) wide.

The petioles themselves are short when exposed to sunlight and lengthen when in subdued light.

The lobes are green when in shadow and red in the sun. Their upper (or

internal) face has three hairs (rarely more) in a triangular formation. They are surrounded by digestive glands, forming a red zone. The periphery of each lobe has a narrow green edging, supplied with nectar-secreting cells that attract insects. The whole is edged with pointed teeth, arranged so that the teeth of one lobe enmesh with those of the other upon closure.

Character. The Venus flytrap is an active plant whose trap is triggered when one of the internal trigger hairs is touched twice or when two hairs of the same leaf are touched. Closure takes place in $\frac{1}{30}$s in sunlight; the speed drops as the temperature falls and also as the leaf becomes older. The lobes are slightly concave and a captive insect can move around inside; if the prey is very small, it can even escape between the teeth, which do not close completely. If, on the other hand, the size of the insect roughly corresponds to that of the trap, the two lobes press against each other with a force big enough to crush some victims. The leaf perishes after capturing four insects in succession.

The double-trigger mechanism avoids the trap closing unnecessarily on something other than a prey, such as falling plant debris; if, despite this, the mechanism triggers off accidentally, the two lobes re-open after about twenty-four hours. The way in which these traps function has been interpreted in several ways, none of which has proved to be entirely satisfactory; transmission of the closure 'command' could be by means of an electrical signal (see Part One – 'Capture and absorption of prey').

Flowers The flower stalks develop in May or June. Each plant has between one and four. The flowers are set in an umbel in groups of two to fifteen; they are regular, star-shaped and have five green sepals, five white petals, and about fifteen stamens. They are 1¼in (3cm) in diameter.

Ornamental effect Exposure to the sun

A Venus flytrap cultivated in sphagnum. The traps are situated at the ends of the petioles. One of them has caught a 'daddy long-legs', a relatively large prey whose legs stick out from the edges of the trap; × 2.5.

Dionaea muscipula

Venus flytrap

colours the interior of the traps a deep red and reduces the length of the petioles. However, if the plants are cultivated under a plastic covering or in a greenhouse, they must not be exposed to the sun, which would scorch them. Plants cultivated in shade stay green and have long or slender petioles. But, however they are exposed, the oldest leaves turn black and, in autumn, all leaves suffer the same fate because of the drop in temperature. Growth returns in spring.

Reproduction

Sexual reproduction Fertilization of the flowers is performed by insects when the plants are outside. To fertilize artificially, take some pollen using a fine brush and transfer it on to the neighbouring flowers of other plants. The stigmas, which have a style divided into five sections, have a sticky appearance when they are ready to be fertilized. Another method is to use fine tweezers to take stamens whose pollen is ripe and to rub them on to the mature pistils, which retain yellow traces of pollen.

The black, shiny seeds reach maturity about five weeks after fertilization. They can be sown immediately or kept in the refrigerator at about 6°. Sow them on them on fine sieved peat. The temperature should be maintained at 12 to 30°C. Germination will be quicker at temperatures above 20°C. The young plants must be thinned out when they become too crowded.

Asexual reproduction. By division: Healthy plants form shoots after several years' growth. When these are sufficiently developed, they can be separated from the mother plant, preferably when repotting.

From leaf cuttings: In summer, the oldest leaves are chosen and the whole of the petiole and the limb used; the cuttings must be planted slanting, with the base of the petioles pushed into the sphagnum or peat. They can also be placed on the soil. They must be kept damp and at a temperature of at least 20°C. The humidity can be increased by placing the culture under a sheet of glass or plastic. The light must be strong. After six or eight weeks small buds form, which give birth to new plants. Each leaf can produce from two to about twenty corms. It is best to transplant them as soon as the roots have developed.

From cuttings from the base of the leaves: The plant at rest is a sort of 'bulb', formed by the base of the old leaves; these turn into scales and the outside ones can be carefully taken off, and used as cuttings in the same way as leaves.

Hybridization

No hybridization has yet been recorded.

Cultivation

Compost The compost can be made from pure sphagnum or pure peat or a mixture of the two. A little river sand may be added. The pH must be kept acid, between 5 and 6. Live sphagnum, which acidifies the water, gives the best results.

Watering For watering, rainwater is recommended, or, if that is not available, distilled water. Water softened with sodium chloride must be avoided.

Also to be avoided are fertilizers, which have disastrous effects – the nitrogen the plant needs is provided by the digestion of insects, never supply morsels of meat – they will simply rot the leaves. In summer, keep the compost moist – water by immersion, placing the base of the pot in water in a shallow container.

Light The Venus flytrap needs as much light as possible and, if in the open air, it can be exposed to full sunlight as long as the temperature does not exceed 37°C.

Temperature The Venus flytrap can withstand slight frost and survives at temperatures of between 0° and 37°C.

Rest Rest is necessary in winter and growth ceases during this period; the plants should for preference be kept at temperatures of between 1° and 12°C; they should be watered in autumn and kept slightly damp over the winter. Blackened leaves should be carefully removed to avoid the spread of *Botrytis*. Plants no longer in leaf should be kept in their pots, ready to be repotted before the growth period returns, or they may be removed from the compost, kept in plastic bags in the refrigerator, and repotted at the right time.

Pests and diseases

Aphids can gather on the flower stalks or, occasionally, on the young leaves, which they can deform. (For treatment, see p.29.)

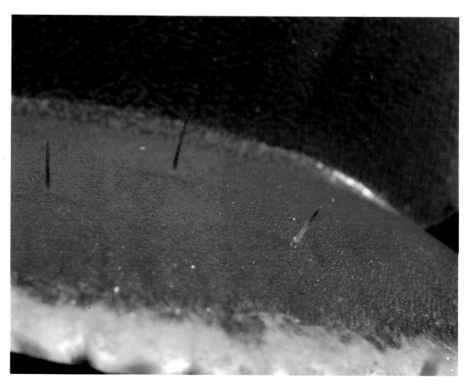

Extremity of a flower stalk, bearing several flowers of different ages.

Left-hand page: the inside face of one lobe of a trap, showing the digestive glands and the three trigger hairs; × 10.

Prey

The size of the prey depends on that of the trap, and therefore on the plant's age. Undersized insects manage to escape through the trap's teeth.

The speed with which this closes allows the capture of even the quickest of insects, such as house flies.

Aldrovanda vesiculosa

Active steel trap

Waterwheel plant

Family Droseraceae.
Genus The genus *Aldrovanda* contains only one species, *A. vesiculosa*.
Common names Waterwheel plant; French, *Plante aquatique á roue;* German, *Wasserfalle*.
Origin India, Asia, North Australia, Japan, Europe.

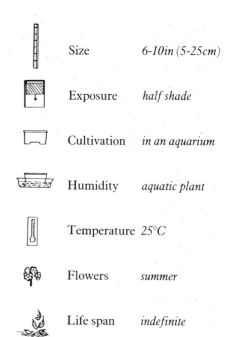

	Size	*6-10in (5-25cm)*
	Exposure	*half shade*
	Cultivation	*in an aquarium*
	Humidity	*aquatic plant*
	Temperature	*25°C*
	Flowers	*summer*
	Life span	*indefinite*

History and etymology

First observed in India in the 16th century, the species was in 1696 described under the name *Lenticula palustris*. It was given its present name in 1747, by the Italian botanist Monti. In 1861, Augé de Lassus noted in the *Bulletin de la Société Botanique de France* that its leaves were sensitive to stimuli and in 1871 Delpino recorded that it caught small fresh-water molluscs. In 1877, Charles Darwin demonstrated its similarity to the Venus flytrap, especially in its method of capturing prey. He called it a 'miniature; aquatic, Venus flytrap' and proved by experiment that it secreted enzymes and digested prey.

The generic name honours the Italian naturalist Ulisse Aldrovandi.

Habitat

Aldrovanda vesiculosa is a floating, though totally immersed, aquatic plant that lives in acidic water in swamps or other types of stagnant water. In warm climates growth is continuous, but the species passes through a winter rest period in cold climates.

Description

Dimensions The species has no roots and is made up of a stem 6-10in (15-25cm) long.
Morphology The plant grows from the apex of the stem and spreads out at the other extremity. In cold regions it changes in autumn into a hibernaculum, or resting bud, and spends the winter submerged at the bottom of the water. The hibernacula rise to the surface in spring and form new plants. The leaves are set in regular rows, in whorls of eight (very occasionally six or nine), looking like the spokes of a wheel around the stalk. They have a flat petiole, wider towards the trap situated at the extremity and about ⅜in (1cm) long.
Character *A. vesiculosa* is an active plant; the structure of its trap is very similiar to that of the Venus flytrap, but in miniature. The trap is formed of two semi-circular lobes, ⅛in (4mm) wide by ¼in (6mm) long, with four to eight cilia, ⁹⁄₁₆in (15mm) long, around its edge. The traps of some species are no more than 1⁄16in (2mm) in length. The outer edge of the lobe has numerous teeth, folded inwards; the interior of each lobe contains about twenty detection hairs that, when excited, activate the closure mechanism in 1⁄50s and make the rest of the plant vibrate. At the base of these hairs are the digestive glands, which

look like tiny marbles. They secrete enzymes and acids that allow the plant to absorb the products of digestion. If it should close accidently, the trap re-opens after a few hours. If the prey is of the right size, the lobes remain tightly closed for several days to allow time for digestion.
Ornamental effect *A. vesiculosa* is a delicate plant, made up of very fine cells that make it seem translucent. Its air pockets allow it to float in the water. It is a natural curiosity, has an unusual structure, and deserves a place in suitable aquariums or in stretches of water having the right level of acidity.
Life span When properly cultivated in a suitable environment the plant develops branches on the main stem. These give rise to new plants, which replace the old ones, so the plant as a whole has an unlimited life span.

Reproduction

Sexual reproduction When the flowers open, they must be fertilized artificaly by taking the pollen from the stamens at the centre of a flower and depositing it on the stigmas. The seeds sow themselves naturally in acid water.
Asexual reproduction The stalk must be cut into sections of 1½-3⅛in (4-8cm), preferably in spring. This type

of cutting allows new shoots to grow, with each part developing into a new plant.

Hybridization

No hybridization has yet been recorded.

Cultivation

Cultivation medium Culture should be in acid water with a pH of between 5 and 6. To obtain acid water in an aquarium, place a thick layer of peat or sphagnum moss, pre-soaked in water, at the bottom of the container. This can be covered with a thin layer of river sand or gravel. This is left to settle for several days, and the floating debris removed, before starting propagation.

To prevent the development of algae, which would stifle the plant, do not use an algicide, which would be dangerous; clean out using a brush. Fertilizers must not be used; on the other hand, it is useful to add daphnia, copepods, or microscopic worms, which will multiply naturally, eliminate algae, and feed the plant.

Light In natural conditions, there is sunlight for several hours per day. In artifical light, during the period of active growth, keep a light intensity of 15,000 to 17,500lx for fourteen to sixteen hours per day.

Temperature The most favourable temperature is 25°C. Exposure to sun must not entail a rise in temperature to above 30°C. Normal growing temperatures are between 20°C and 30°C in summer. If continual growth is required, the water temperature must not drop below 17 °C.

Pests and diseases

No disease is known. The only pests are microscopic algae, which can stifle the plants.

Part of the stem of *Aldrovanda vesiculosa*, showing two whorls, each having eight leaves. The end of each leaf is modified into a trap, as in the Venus flytrap. The prey is aquatic, to suit the plant's natural environment; × 19.

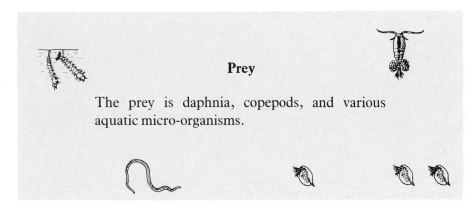

Prey

The prey is daphnia, copepods, and various aquatic micro-organisms.

Active mousetrap

*U*tricularia vulgaris

Greater bladderwort

Family Lentibulariaceae.
Genus The genus *Utricularia* comprises about 275 species.
Common games Greater bladderwort, hooded water milfoil; French, *Mille-feuilles des marais;* German, *Wasserhelm, Wasserschlauch, Schlauchkraut;* Italian, *Millefolio acquatico, erba vescica, ava di botta.*
Origin Europe, Siberia, North Africa, North America (including Alaska).

	Size	4-10in (10-25cm)
	Exposure	half shade
	Cultivation	in an aquarium or a pond
	Humidity	aquatic plant
	Temperature	0° to 30°C
	Flowers	May to September
	Life span	indefinite

History and etymology

The *Utricularia* were first classified, by botanists who had noticed that they caught fry, as piscivores. Later, Darwin pointed out the remains of worms, crustaceans, and other small animals in the traps. It was only in 1876, though, that Mary Treat discovered that victims were pulled into the traps by suction. The presence of enzymes, and therefore of digestive activity, was proved in 1910.

Habitat

Utricularia vulgaris lives in ditches, ponds, marshes, or even peat bogs. The plant is submerged and the flowering parts emerge above the surface only in summer.

Description

Dimensions The stalk, floating near the surface, can reach 13ft (4mm) in length. The flower stalks are 4-12in (10-30cm) high. In winter, the plant forms hibernacula of about ½in (12mm) diameter.
Morphology In summer, the plant comprises one slender and very long stalk, which bears branches with numerous leaves. In winter, the plant is reduced to the hibernacula, consisting of small leaves assembled into a compact bundle. These leaves are covered in very fine hairs. The hibernacula spend the winter on the bottom, in spring, due to an absorption of gases dissolved in the water, they return to the surface and are the beginnings of the plant's summertime development.
Character *U. vulgaris* is an active plant. The traps, called bladders, are fixed to the leaves by a very small stalk. They are small pockets, compressed laterally, and the size of a grain of pepper. At first they are white or transparent so that the prey is visible inside; they then darken with age. They have a mouth, hermetically sealed when at rest, and glands that discharge water to maintain the internal pressure below that of the surrounding water. The mouth is surrounded by very fine antennae, which comprise several branches forming a funnel. This serves to guide the prey towards the entrance

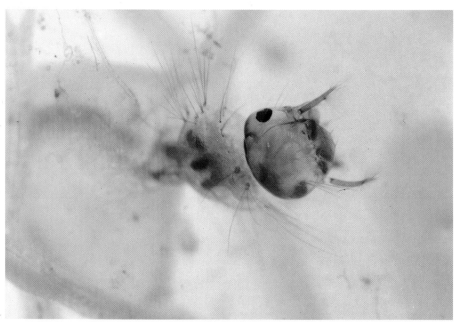

of the trap; prey are then detected by cilia which also, at the slightest touch, give the command for the mouth to close. This particularly rapid reflex ($\frac{1}{50}$ to $\frac{1}{500}$s) causes a sudden flood of water into the utricle, thereby bringing up the internal pressure of the trap to the same level as that of the surroundings. At the same time, the prey is sucked into the trap and the mouth immediately closes. Water is then emptied slowly, but the prey remains enclosed in the bladder. Digestion takes place under the twin action of enzymes and bacteria. The trap is ready for action again after about 60min. If the prey is too large to be absorbed in one go, which happens for example with mosquito larvae, the mouth stretches around it like a piece of elastic and the suction procedure is repeated several times until absorption is complete. Even larger prey are kept away from the trigger hairs by the antennae at the entrance.

Utricularia vulgaris is a carnivorous plant that floats just under the surface of the water. The leaves are divided into folioles, which bear the traps. Prey, captured by suction, is small, aquatic animalcules like this mosquito larva (left); × 25.

A mosquito larva imprisoned in the mouth of a bladderwort's utricle; × 36.

Utricularia vulgaris

Active mousetrap

Greater bladderwort

Flowers The erect flower stalks bear two to ten pedunculate flowers, arranged in a simple bunch. The bright yellow corolla consists of a coneshaped spur. It flowers from May to September.
Ornamental effect *U. vulgaris* floats under the surface of the water. It has fine, dark green foliage and its flowers, which last throughout the summer, are very beautiful.
Life span The life span of the species is indefinite : each plant produces hibernacula and so can survive from year to year.

Utricularia vulgaris in flower. Note the transparent utricles; × 1.8.

Reproduction

Sexual reproduction The species does not seem to be autogamous and artificial means must be used to obtain seeds. These mature in autumn and must be placed in a plastic bag or in a glass tube in the refrigerator. They are then simply sown on the surface of the water. Germination takes about two months.
Asexual reproduction Simply cut the stalk of the mature plant into segments 2-4in (5-10cm) long; each one, when placed in the water, produces a new plant.

Hybridization

No hybridization has been recorded for the genus *Utricularia*.

Cultivation

Cultivation medium Like all aquatic species of its genus, *U. vulgaris* can be cultivated in all kinds of aquariums or even in natural or artificial ponds outdoors. In all cases, peat or sphagnum is placed on the bottom, to a depth of 1-8in (2-20cm), wetting it first in order to weigh it down, otherwise it may rise to the surface. The pH of the water must be maintained between 4.5 and 6. If the water is not sufficiently acid, more peat or sphagnum can be used. The pH can also be lowered by adding (drop by drop) very small amounts of phosphoric, nitric, or sulphuric acid. (Remember that these are dangerous chemicals.) Check the rise in acidity with a pH meter. On the other hand, to raise the pH, add chalk, ammonium, or potash. Too alkaline a water carries the risk of the spread of algae. To eliminate them, an American horticulturist, Pietropaolo, recommends using copper sulphate in small doses in the following proportions: dissolve 1g of crystallized or powdered copper sulphate in 5.4l of water and use 7.5ml of this solution for every litre in the propagation container. Do not increase this amount or you may kill the plants. A more natural method of getting rid of algae is to introduce daphnia, copepods, or microscopic worms into the water; these organisms, which are easily purchased, or found in forest ponds, multiply rapidly.

Light An appropriate intensity of light is equivalent to 50 per cent of solar light. Exposure to full sunlight encourages the development of algae. In artificial light, in summer, an intensity of 5,000 to 10,0001x must be maintained. In winter, the hibernacula need no light.

Temperature *U. vulgaris* is a species from temperate climates and can withstand winter frosts. Temperatures should be between 0° and 14°C during this season and between 12° and 30°C during the summer.

Rest Shorter daylight hours and a drop in temperature stimulate the beginning of the rest period. Hibernacula form when the temperature drops below 7°C. They fall to the bottom and thus avoid being trapped in the ice. Outdoors, any water containing butterworts must therefore be deep enough not to freeze completely.

Pests and diseases

Aphids may sometimes attack the flowers above the surface. (For treatment, see p.29.)

Related species

The two species of the former genus *Biovularia* (now reclassified as *Utricularia*), which are not cultivated, show a great morphological similiarity to *U. vulgaris*. (See also p.140 for the list of species of the genus *Utricularia*.)

Two beautiful flowers at the top of the stalk of a butterwort. Because the flower is above water – it is the only part of the plant that is – pollination has to be by aerial means; × 5.5.

Uses and properties

Ancient medicine attributed diuretic properties to the bladderwort.

Prey

Because of the plant's life style, its prey is, naturally enough, aquatic animals – small crustaceans (daphnia, copepods), worms and the aquatic larvae of small insects.

*U*tricularia sandersonii

Active mousetrap

Family Lentibulariaceae.
Genus The genus *Utricularia* comprises about 275 species.
Origin South Africa.

	Size	1½-2⁵⁄₁₆in (4-6cm) flower stalk
	Exposure	half shade
	Cultivation	in pots
	Humidity	variable
	Temperature	6° to 30°C
	Flowers	nearly all year
	Life Span	indefinite

Etymology

The specific name honours F. Sander, an English importer and horticulturist at the end of the last century.

Habitat

Utricularia sandersonii is a terrestrial plant that grows in marshy areas where it is shaded by surrounding vegetation.

Description

Dimensions It is a dwarf plant whose leaves measure only ⅛-¼in (3-6mm) long. Its fine and slender flower stalks are 1½-2¼in (4-6cm) high.
Morphology The leaves, shaped like elongated spatulas, are of pale green colour. They grow just above the soil.
Character The traps, or bladders, are borne on underground stems. They are small vesicles, hermetically sealed when at rest, armed with detection hairs around the mouth. When a potential prey touches one of these, the bladder's orifice opens suddenly, dragging the victim in through the suction created. This mechanism can function only in very wet soil. Bacteria and enzymes together are responsible for the digestion of the prey.

The long, upward-curving spur is a particular feature of the flower of *Utricularia sandersonii*; × 5.

Flowers The slender flower stalk bears one to seven flowers. These are ¼-⁹⁄₁₆in (6-14mm) in diameter and have an upper lip (formed by the upper petals) divided into two lobes with violet markings near the centre. The lower lip (made up of the lower petals) is twice as long and, dropping downwards as it does, make a kind of wavy-edged apron. The palate, at the centre of the flower, is yellowy-green, becoming violet towards the edge. The spur, a sort of cylindrical tube situated in the lower part of the flower, is long and curved.
Ornamental effect *U. sandersonii* flowers prolifically and its delicate blooms are most attractive.
Life span Its life span is indefinite since it is able continually to multiply its underground stems.

Reproduction

Sexual reproduction The flowers are autogamous, which means that they can fertilize themselves. They produce large quantities of seeds, which are sown naturally around the mother plant. If this process is allowed to continue, it produces a dense carpet of numerous plants and hence a large and almost continuous show of flowers.
Asexual reproduction The tufts may be divided, each fragment then being separately replanted. Care should be taken to lift the roots complete with a clump of soil.

Hybridization

There are no known hybrids of *Utricularia*.

Cultivation

Compost The most appropriate compost is peat, sphagnum, or a mixture of the two. One third river sand may be added. The pH must be maintained between 4.5 and 6.
Compost The compost must be kept very damp during the whole of the growth period. Water when necessary by placing the pot in a shallow bath of

A culture of *Utricularia sandersonii* in flower. This is a terrestrial species, so the traps are situated beneath the surface of the soil; × 3.

water. This moisture is vital to growth and to the operation of the bladders. They should be kept slightly damp during the winter to avoid dehydration.

Light An intensity of light equivalent to 50 per cent of sunlight is required by *U. sandersonii*. For artificial light, this corresponds to an intensity of between 5,000 and 10,000lx in summer and between 1,000 and 3,000lx in winter.
Temperature *U. sandersonii* is a subtropical species, so the ranges of temperature appropriate for its cultivation are from 16° to 30°C in summer and from 6° to 18°C in winter.

Pests and diseases

Two types of trouble must be watched for – aphids, and fungi of the genus *Oïdium*. (For treatment, see pp.28–9.)

Closely related species

See the list of species of the genus *Utricularia* on p. 140.

Prey

The prey is animalcules that live in waterlogged soils – protozoans or rotifers and other small worms.

Utricularia alpina

Mountain Utricularia

Family Lentibulariaceae.
Genus The genus *Utricularia* comprises about 275 species.
Common name Mountain Utricularia.
Origin Central and South America (Columbia, Guyana, Peru, Venezuela), West Indies (Dominica, Martinique, Saint Vincent, La Trinité, Grenada).

	Size	8-12 in (20-30 cm) flower stalk
	Exposure	half shade
	Cultivation	in a pot or hanging basket
	Humidity	average
	Temperature	6° to 30°C
	Flowers	summer
	Life span	indefinite

Etymology

Both specific names, *alpina* and *montana*, are purely descriptive, recognizing that the plant is a mountain dweller.

Habitat

Utricularia alpina is an epiphytic species – it lives on trees that grow on the mountains at heights frequently covered by clouds. The plant grows on mosses that develop on the branches. It develops on the side with the most light.

Description

Dimensions The leaves are 4-6in (10-15cm) long and the flower stalks 8-12in (20-30cm) in height.
Morphology *U. alpina* is a creeper – it bears rhizomes which spread out in all directions. Its tubers are ³⁄₈-1in (1-2.5cm) in length. Oblong in shape, these are white or transparent, becoming greenish with age or fully green when exposed to light. They form a food reserve that the plant uses in dry periods. The long leaves grow up from these creeping rhizomes; spear-headed in shape, fleshy, and with a barely visible vein, they are deep green in colour.

Character The bladders are like small waterskins with trap-like openings surrounded by very fine antennae. When the antennae detect a potential prey, the trap opens suddenly, creating suction because at rest the internal pressure of the trap is lower than that of the surroundings – which forces the victim inside the bladder, where it is digested by enzymes and bacteria.
Flowers The slender flower stalk bears one to four flowers whose calyx comprises two pale yellow sepals. The white corolla, 1³⁄₈in (3.5cm) wide, is composed of a labellum – a well-developed petal forming the lower part of the flower. The labellum is yellow at its base, becoming white as it widens towards the front of the flower. The

The stolons of *Utricularia alpina*, bearing the trap or bladders. Below, a tuber, which acts as a water store; × 4.

corolla also has a trumpet-shaped spur, 1¼in (3cm) long. Curving upwards at the front, this is situated under the labellum and extends beyond it. The two stamens are right inside the flower and the sessile stigma overhangs the spherical ovary.
Ornamental effect The flowers of *U. alpina* are reminiscent of those of certain orchids. White in colour, they are tinged to a greater or lesser extent with pink and turn yellow with age.
Life span Life expectancy is unlimited, the rhizomes ensuring the continuation of the species.

Reproduction

Sexual reproduction The species does not seem to be autogamous. To reach the anthers and the stigma in order to fertilize the flowers, it is necessary to separate carefully their upper and lower lips. When mature, the seeds are placed in the refrigerator in a plastic bag or glass tube and then sown on wet, sifted peat in spring.

Asexual reproduction The plant can be reproduced by selecting mature specimens and separating the leaves along with their respective portions of the stolon.

Hybridization

No known hybrid exists.

Cultivation

Compost Several composts are suitable – sphagnum, peat, the roots or fronds of ferns of the genus *Platycerium*, and orchid composts can equally well be used. All kinds of containers are suitable, too – plastic or clay pots, as well as perforated or slatted hanging baskets, give excellent results.

Watering The compost must remain damp throughout the growing period; the atmosphere must also be kept sufficiently humid. However, water less during winter.

Light The temperature must be kept between 16° and 30°C in summer, and between 6° and 18°C in winter.

Pests and diseases

Always be prepared for attack by aphids or fungus. (For treatment, see pp.28–9.)

Related species

See p.140 for the list of species of the genus *Utricularia*.

A few mountain *Utricularia* stems, out of their pot. Amid the tangle of stolons, the small bladders can be distinguished (top right of the root system). The thicker, rather inflated, parts are the tubers; × 1.

Prey

Although the bladders are relatively large, their size, less than ³⁄₁₆in (5mm), limits that of potential prey. Victims are small invertebrates living in the moss where the plant's rhizomes grow.

Active fly-paper trap

Drosera binata

Forked-leaved sundew

Family Droseraceae.
Genus The genus *Drosera* comprises more than 100 species.
Common names Forked- or twin-leaved sundew; French, *Rossolis à feuilles bifurquées.*
Origin Eastern and southeastern Australia (New South Wales, Victoria, Tasmania), New Zealand.

Size	*up to 20in (50cm)*	
Exposure	*light shade or full sun*	
Cultivation	*in pots*	
Humidity	*constant*	
Temperature	*moderate*	
Flowers	*spring*	
Life span	*indefinite*	

Etymology

The specific name *binata* has been attributed to the plant because of the bipartite or Y-shaped division of its leaves.

Habitat

Drosera binata can be found in situations ranging from mountain bogs to low-altitude swamps, but always in a constantly wet, acid soil.

Description

Dimensions The plant can reach 20in (50cm) in height.
Morphology The leaves are radical and very narrow, with long petioles, and are divided into two long Y-shaped blades; they are smooth underneath and have numerous glandular hairs on the upper surfaces and the sides. The stalks are two to four times longer than the blades; they are bare and semi-cylindrical. Leaf division may be simple or repeated.
Character *D. binata* is a semi-active plant that captures its prey by means of numerous, well-developed tentacles.
Flowers The flower stalks are erect and higher than the leaves; they are dichotomous, with a short panicle. The edges of the flower calyx have fine cilia or are toothed at the top. The white petals are oval like the ovary. The styles are grouped in threes or fives.
Ornamental effect This species, along with its sub-species, is distinguishable by its Y-shaped foliage, with each leaf dividing into two branches.
Life span Indefinite: the plant stops growing when it experiences a cold spell and re-emerges from the rhizomes when warmth returns.

Reproduction

Sexual reproduction *D. binata* is not a self-fertilizing species, so, to obtain seeds, the pollen from one plant must be deposited (with a brush or feather) on the stigmas of another. The fruit is ripe when it turns black. The capsules should be cut off, along with the flower stalks, and placed in envelopes. They will release tiny seeds, which must be subjected to cold – kept in the refrigerator at between 2° and 7°C, until spring or at least until February. Propagating trays should then be prepared, filled with peat, finely sieved on the surface, and the whole tray steeped in a shallow bath of water. Water with a fungicide and sow the seeds on the surface. If the medium is kept permanently damp, germination begins in a few weeks. As soon as the small plants become a little crowded, they must be replanted into similar trays so that they can develop normally.
Asexual reproduction *D. binata* can be reproduced from leaf cuttings or, better still, from root cuttings. One or several roots can be taken as long as this does not damage the mother plant. They should be cut into about 1in (2-3cm) sections and pushed gently into the seed trays. Cultivation conditions are the same as those for leaf cuttings (see *Drosera filiformis*: 'Asexual reproduction').

Hybridization

D. binata up till now does not seem to have been hybridized with other species.

Cultivation

Compost Like other species of *Drosera* from temperate climates, *D. binata* does best in pure sphagnum, pure peat, or a mixture of the two substrates. To this may be added some vermiculite, perlite, or river sand, in the proportion of 1/10 to 1/5 of the total amount of compost. The pH must be acid, between 4.5 and 5.5.
Watering Keep the compost damp, slightly less so in winter.
Light In a greenhouse, diffused light

Drosera binata in cultivation. The very narrow leaves have numerous, long, glandular tentacles. Insects can be seen, glued to the leaves.

equivalent to 50 per cent of sunlight is ideal for *D. binata*.

Temperature *D. binata* is a plant suited to temperate greenhouses or it can be grown outdoors, provided it is protected from frost. When at rest, the species can withstand temperatures as low as 3°C.

Rest The leaves blacken and disappear at the onset of the cold season. New growth usually occurs after two to four months, at most after five. It is during the rest period that repotting should take place. Note that the *D. binata* var. *multifida* can be kept growing without a rest period if the temperature does not fall below 18°C.

Pests and diseases

The most frequently seen pest is the aphid, which thrives especially on the flower stalks. Red spiders, mealy bugs, and scale insects rarely attack *Drosera*. Be wary of *Botrytis*, which must be treated immediately. Certain caterpillars can feed on *Drosera* without becoming trapped, but they are easy to detect. (For treatment, see pp.28-31)

Varieties and closely related species

D. binata var. *dichotoma* is characterized by its relatively large size and spread. Its doubly branched leaves are H-shaped. In *D. binata* var. *multifida*, the leaves have four to eight branches. (See also p.138 for the list of species of *Drosera* from temperate climates.)

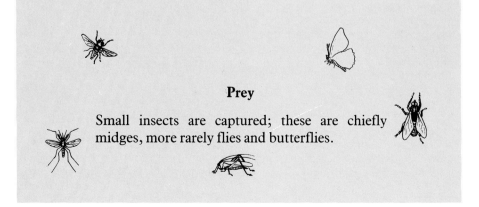

Prey

Small insects are captured; these are chiefly midges, more rarely flies and butterflies.

Drosera capensis

Active fly-paper trap

Cape sundew

Family Droseraceae.
Genus The genus *Drosera* comprises more than 100 species.
Common names Cape sundew; French, *Drosera du Cap*.
Origin Cape Province, South Africa.

Size		2¾-6in (7-15cm)
Exposure		*full sunlight or half shade*
Cultivation		*in pots or in terraria*
Humidity		*high*
Temperature		*2° to 40°C*
Flowers		*spring*
Life span		*unlimited*

Etymology

The name of the species simply refers to its native region.

Habitat

In its natural state, *Drosera capensis* lives in marshy, spongy, peaty soils, among grasses. The species can withstand full sunlight and must be given as much sunlight as possible. The best place to cultivate it indoors is in a window, in a pot or terrarium, kept constantly humid, though rather less so in winter.

Description

Dimensions A hardy plant, it measures 2¾-6in (7-15cm) in height when fully grown. The petiole can reach 1½in (4cm) and the leaf is 4in (10cm) long and ⅛-¼in (4-6mm) wide. The flower stalks can grow to 12in (30cm) and bear four to twenty pink flowers, ¾in (2cm) in diameter. The rosette of leaves is roughly 6in (15cm) in diameter.
Morphology Older plants grow longer stems. The narrow leaves are capable of movement, not only the glandular hairs but also the limb, which folds over in order to hold the prey when captured, pushing it on to the digestive glands situated mainly in the centre of the leaves. The foliage completely disappears in winter if the plant is subject to low temperatures of about 2° to 10°C.
Character The glandular hairs turn and fold towards the captured prey. The movement is very slow but quite visible. It continues for a period of anything between six and fourteen hours, according to the vigour of the plant and to the temperature. Activity increases with a rise in temperature and in intensity of light.
Flowers The flowers are set along one side of a stalk, opening one after the other from the base. They are a beautiful pink colour and the stalks offer an extra attraction. After flowering, the stalks remain erect in order to carry the brown capsules containing the seeds.
Ornamental effect The plant itself is very decorative and looks magnificent when viewed against the light, its white and red glands gleaming in the sun.
Life span The life span is unlimited, especially as vigorous plants form shoots on the rhizomes that produce, in turn, tufts of many other plants.

Reproduction

Sexual reproduction The seeds sow themselves, giving rise to many small plants in spring. Simply prick them out and put them in trays, then in pots. One can also collect the seeds and leave them to dehydrate between two sheets of paper. They are then kept cold over winter, either outside or in a refrigerator, at a temperature of 5°to7°C, before sowing them in spring in trays of fine peat, kept moist. Humidity can be maintained by covering the seedbed with a sheet of glass or plastic, and placing it in natural light. Instead of peat, chopped and sieved sphagnum moss can be used. It is best to scald the sphagnum beforehand to avoid the risk of it spreading and suffocating the seedbeds. As soon as the seedlings have germinated, they must be pricked out and placed in the same medium (preferably peat), and thinned out. Thinning can be in staggered or straight lines. Use the point of a small stick for this, dipping it in water each time, so that the seedling sticks to it and is more easily placed on the surface of the peat. Water copiously before thinning out and thereafter water preferably by immersion or by light and repeated spraying. Prior treatment with a fungicide is recommended. This can be applied when watering the seed tray, before thinning out. Thereafter, one need only spray the surface once the first shoot has appeared. The plants will mature fully after three years of cultivation.
Asexual reproduction This is possible

by taking cuttings and placing them either in seed trays or by cultivating them in vitro in a medium of agar-agar, as for orchids. A leaf fragment or any other part of the plant is able to regenerate cells which give birth to new plants, identical to the mother plant. Fragments of the underground rhizome can regenerate in the same way. Place the cuttings on the surface of the peat. It is best to soak them in a fungicide before putting them in place. They are then treated in the same way as those grown from seed.

Hybridization

Pollination in *D. capensis* occurs automatically through the closing of the flower after its flowering period. But artificial fertilization is necessary if you wish to cross it with another species of *Drosera*. Watch the flower carefully and take off the petals as soon as they develop. Remove also the stamens around the stigma, to avoid any risk of self-fertilization. Take the pollen from the stamens of the chosen plant with a watercolour paintbrush and put them into contact with the stigma of the mother plant.

Cultivation

Compost *D. capensis* is a species from peat bogs. It is a vigorous plant and easy to cultivate in pots or terraria. A sphagnum-moss or peat compost allows the water to be maintained at a pH of 5 or 5.5.
Watering *D. capensis* does not mind an excess of water in summer; the pots can therefore remain in a bath of water in order to avoid any dehydration. Rainwater is best.

Light Beautiful plants are obtained by exposing them to the sun, but those cultivated in the shade are also quite healthy, although there is less red pigmentation and the leaves are more tender.
Temperature The temperature should be kept at over 2°C in winter, but there is virtually no upper limit (up to 40 °C) in summer. Cultivation outdoors is possible except during frosts, which may kill the plant. If, however, the frost is only slight, the underground rhizome allows growth to re-appear in spring.
Rest Keep the plant moderately damp in winter during the rest period.

Pests and diseases

This species harbours very few pests. Nevertheless, keep an eye open for aphids, which may settle on the flower stalks.

Related species
See p.138 for the list of species of *Drosera* from temperate climates.

A fine example of *Drosera capensis*. Its original effect comes both from the flowers and from the red tentacles tipped with glassy globules; × 0.5.

Prey

The usual prey of *D. capensis* is small Diptera of the genus *Sciara*. On rare occasions a spider may be caught. Flies and mosquitoes are sometimes trapped.

Active fly-paper trap

Drosera filiformis

Threadleaf sundew

Family Droseraceae.
Genus The genus *Drosera* comprises more than 100 species.
Common names Threadleaf sundew or dew thread; French, *Rossolis filiforme*.
Origin North America (Atlantic coast from Cape Cod to south of Mississippi).

	Size	*10-20in (25-50cm)*
	Exposure	*light shade or full sun*
	Cultivation	*in pots*
	Humidity	*constant*
	Temperature	*3° to 40°C*
	Flowers	*spring*
	Life Span	*indefinite*

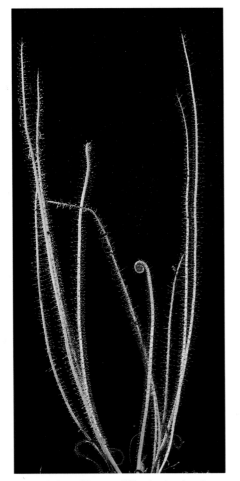

General view of *Drosera filiformis*, showing the slender nature of its leaves × 0.8.

Etymology

The name of the species, *filiformis*, comes from the structure of its long and slender leaves.

Habitat

The botanist Pursh left this description of the species, reported in Diderot's *Encyclopédie*: 'This plant grows amongst pines in the sandy, marshy regions of New Jersey. It occupies large areas and produces a marvellous show of flowers.' The plant still grows wild in large numbers in peat or sphagnum moss.

Description

Dimensions The leaves are about 10in (25cm) in height.
Morphology In winter, the plant reduces to a hibernaculum wrapped in a woolly shell. In spring, small, shiny leaves appear, wide at the base and terminating in a point. Subsequent leaves, rolled up like a scroll, gradually develop – they are narrow, linear and silvery in appearance. The petiole is very short and merges with the blade.
Character *Drosera filiformis* is a semi-active plant. The leaves are covered with red or green glandular tentacles, the longest of which capture numerous insects, which are then absorbed by the digestive glands.
Flowers The erect flower stalks stand clear of the foliage. They are smooth and cylindrical in section. The flowers are set unilaterally on curved stalks. They are pink in colour and are 9/16-3/4in (1.5-2cm) in diameter according to the variety.
Ornamental effect The ornamental effect is very striking because of the brilliance of the glands and the silvery tint of the whole plant, reminiscent of certain lichens. It is an elegant plant, with its long, slender, erect leaves.
Life span Indefinite.

Reproduction

Sexual reproduction *D. filiformis* is a self-fertilizing species, so seeds can be obtained without the need for outside intervention. Simply cut the flower stalk when it blackens in order to collect the seeds. These should be kept in the cold (between 2° and 7°C), then sown at the beginning of spring on trays filled with wet peat (see *D. binata*: 'Sexual reproduction').
Asexual reproduction Cuttings can be taken from the roots, but those from the leaves are better. The whole leaf is used,

A flower of *Drosera filiformis*, on the very end of its stalk. Other flowers are just forming; × 3.

complete with all the petiole. It is immersed for a few minutes in a solution of fungicide. The base is then pushed into peat or into chopped and very wet sphagnum. Watering with a fungicide solution will complete the treatment against possible fungus attack. The propagating tray should then be kept constantly damp. This can be done by covering it with a sheet of glass or by transparent plastic sheeting, held up in the centre by a stick, so that the sides slope enough to ensure that condensation falls around the tray and not on the cuttings. This arrangement means that watering is not needed for several weeks. The temperature must be kept between 18° and 26°C. The young plants grow at the base of the petiole or on the limb, just under the surface of the compost.

Hybridization

D. filiformis can be hybridized with *D. intermedia* to give *D. × hybrida*.

Cultivation

Compost The pH must be maintained between 4.5 and 5.5 by using sphagnum, peat, or a mixture of the two. Small quantities of vermiculite, perlite, or river sand may be added.

Watering The compost must always remain damp during the growing period. The water must be as pure as possible and rainwater should preferably be used. It is advisable not to use water containing calcium or chlorine, such as that produced by water softeners that use sodium chloride.

Light Especially in the greenhouse, *D. filiformis* should be given shade, so that the temperature does not rise too high. But too much shade may make the plant wilt. On the other hand, sunlight tends to colour the leaves red, which attracts more insects, and also favours the development of flowers.

Temperature This must be between 12° and 40°C in summer.

Rest *D. filiformis* spends the winter in the form of a hibernaculum; it must be kept at rest and cold (between 3° and 7°C) for three to five months, in slightly damp conditions.

Detail of a leaf of *Drosera filiformis*, illustrating the efficiency of the traps; × 3.5.

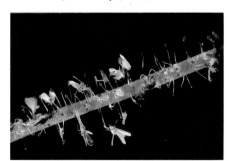

A young leaf, sporting especially glistening tentacles; × 9.

Pests and diseases

The main problem is aphids and *Botrytis* (For treatment, see pp.28–9.)

Closely related species

The subspecies *D. filiformis tracyi* is distinguished from the species by its larger size and, in particular, by the greater diameter – ¾in (2cm) – of its flowers. (See also p.138 for the list of *Drosera* species of temperate climates.)

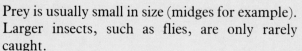

Prey

Prey is usually small in size (midges for example). Larger insects, such as flies, are only rarely caught.

Drosera rotundifolia

Active fly-paper trap

Roundleaf sundew

Family Droseraceae.
Genus The genus *Drosera* comprises more than 100 species.
Common names Roundleaf sundew; French, *Rossolis à feuilles rondes*.
Origin America (northern United States and Canada), Asia, Europe. This is probably the most widespread carnivorous species in the world.

	Size	*4-4¾in (10-12cm) in diameter*
	Exposure	*light shade or full sun*
	Cultivation	*in pots*
	Humidity	*constant*
	Temperature	*to 40 °C*
	Flowers	*spring*
	Life span	*indefinite*

Etymology

The round shape of the leaf limb explains the specific name. A 17th-century French botanist, Joseph Pitton de Tournefort, had earlier named it 'Rossolis folio rotundo'.

Habitat

This species of *Drosera* grows in damp, marshy, acid areas, often in the presence of sphagnum moss.

Description

Dimensions The leaf petiole is ¾-2in (2.5cm) long, while the limb, rather more wide than long, has an average diameter of ¼-⅜in (6-10mm). The flower stalks themselves are 2-8in (5-20cm) long.
Morphology The roots are fine, fibrous, and blackish. The numerous leaves, in rosette formation, are radical and prostrate, with the new leaves covering the old ones. The petiole has fewer cilia than the left blade, which is slightly hollow towards the centre. These glandular hairs are longer at the outer edge of the limb and they turn red on exposure to the sun. *Drosera rotundifolia* is a perennial plant : with the cooler

temperatures of autumn and winter the leaves blacken and the plant gradually reduces into a hibernaculum.
Character Any insect caught in the mucilage of one or more tentacles stimulates the neighbouring tentacles, which fold in towards the prey; the limb itself bends over to further enclose the victim, surrounding it with copious amounts of mucilage and bringing it slowly towards the centre of the leaf, where the digestive glands are situated.

Drosera rotundifolia: capture mechanism; × 3.5.

Flowers The flower stalks rise from the centre of the rosette. They are smooth, cylindrical, simple or double. The white flowers, often pink on the American continent, may be single or in groups containing up to twenty flowers. Their stalks are short and stand upright after flowering. The calyx comprises five oval, slightly pointed lobes. The corolla, barely longer then the calyx, is formed of five petals, also oval in shape. Each flower contains five stamens and, usually, three styles. The seed pod comprises one compartment, opening into five valves at the top. The seeds are small and slightly tuberous.
Ornamental effect Despite its small size, the plant is a favourite of collectors. It is a plant curiosity, which gains most of its beauty from the red hues it easily acquires when subjected to intense light.
Life span Indefinite.

Reproduction

Sexual reproduction The flowers reproduce by self-fertilization. When the flower stalk blackens it should be cut and the seed pods, together with their seeds, collected. The seeds should spend the winter in the cold (between 2° and 7°C) and be sown in spring in seed trays filled with peat and kept permanently damp. When the seedlings become too crowded, they are pricked out into other trays.

Asexual reproduction It is possible to reproduce *D. rotundifolia* by leaf cuttings. Use the whole leaf. After soaking the leaf for a few minutes in a fungicide solution, gently push the cut end as far as the petiole into peat or damp sphagnum. Then water with a fungicide solution and keep the medium moist. Simpler still, whole leaves can be floated on the surface of the water and left to reproduce. The cut part of the leaf may be first treated with hormones, but this is not absolutely necessary.

Hybridization

D. rotundifolia hybridizes naturally with *D. anglica* to give *D. × obovata*.

Cultivation

Compost Sphagnum, peat, or a mixture of the two can be used. Very small proportions of vermiculite, perlite, or river sand may be added. The pH must be between 4.5 and 5.5.

Watering The compost must always be wet. If possible, rainwater should be used; water containing calcium or chlorine must be avoided.

Light In natural conditions, *D. rotundifolia* appreciates full sun or light shade. In artificial light, 10,000 to 15,000lx should be given for a period of fourteen to sixteen hours per day in summer, this being progressively reduced during autumn to drop to 8,500lx for eight to twelve hours per day in winter.

Temperature *D. rotundifolia* is a hardy plant – when dominant it can withstand sub-zero temperatures. On the other hand, the maximum temperature must never exceed 40°C.

Rest This species spends the winter in the form of a hibernaculum or kind of scaly bud. Leave it to rest at a temperature of between 3° and 7°C.

Pests and diseases

D. rotundifolia is especially vulnerable to aphids and fungus. (For treatment, see pp.28–9.)

Related species

See p.138 for the list of *Drosera* from temperate climates.

A young *Drosera rotundifolia* plant. Its rounded leaves are prostrate; × 5.5.

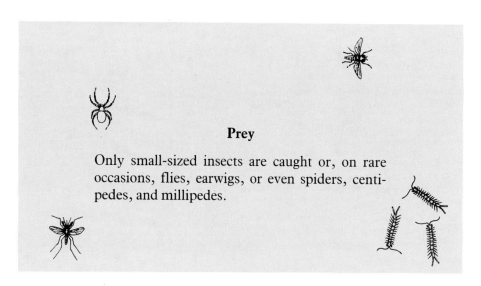

Prey

Only small-sized insects are caught or, on rare occasions, flies, earwigs, or even spiders, centipedes, and millipedes.

Active fly-paper trap

Drosera spathulata

Spoonleaf sundew

Family Droseraceae.
Genus The genus *Drosera* comprises more than 100 species.
Common names Spoonleaf sundew; French *Rossolis spatulé*.
Origin Asia, Australia (New South Wales, Queensland, Victoria, Tasmania), Borneo, China, Hong Kong, Japan, New Zealand, Philippines, Taiwan.

Size		2¼-10in (6-25cm) flower stalk
Exposure		full sun
Cultivation		in pots
Humidity		constant
Temperature		15° to 30°C
Flowers		spring to summer
Life span		indefinite

Etymology

The name *spathulata*, given by the botanist Labillardière in 1804, refers to the shape of the leaves, which are like spatulas or spoons.

Habitat

Drosera spathulata grows in marshy or less damp places, in an acid soil.

Description

Dimensions The leaves comprise a petiole ⅜-¾in (1-2cm) in length, which gradually widens into a limb, ⅜-1in (1-2.5cm) long. The flower stalks, in the centre of the plant, are 2¼-10in (6-25cm) long.
Morphology The radical leaves are set in rosette formation; their limbs are spatula-shaped, with variations according to origin and variety.
Character The glandular hairs that capture the prey adorn the top and the edge of the limb.
Flowers The flower stalks bear two to eighteen white or pink flowers according to the variety. The sepals, ³⁄₁₆in (5mm) long, are almost rectangular; the petals are larger and rounded, and the stamens half as long as these. There are three twin styles, curving upwards; they are the same size as the stamens. The oval

seed pod, containing three or five valves, has numerous fine, black, elliptical seeds.
Ornamental effect *D. spathulata* is a small-sized species. The spatula-shaped leaf blade and the numerous brightly coloured tentacles, give this plant its ornamental value.
Life span Indefinite. Growth is continuous in conditions corresponding to those of the natural habitat.

Reproduction

Sexual reproduction *D. spathulata* reproduces by self-fertilization, so seeds can be obtained without the need to transfer pollen from one flower to another. The seeds must be kept in the cold before being sown in the trays (see *Drosera binata*: Sexual reproduction).
Asexual reproduction Leaf cuttings of *D. spathulata* can certainly be taken, but it is a species that reproduces more readily from root cuttings. One or a number of roots can be taken from a mother plant without damaging it. These are then cut into about 1in (2-3cm) segments and lightly pushed into seed trays containing peat or chopped sphagnum. Water first with a fungicide solution to pre-empt the formation of fungi; the compost should then be kept moist.

Hybridization

D. spathulata can hybridize with *D. anglica* to give *D.* × *nagamoto*.

Cultivation

Compost Although *D. spathulata* is a tropical species, the cultivation compost should be the same as that for temperate-climate species: peat and sphagnum, used separately or mixed, are suitable.
Watering The medium must be kept permanently damp but not turned into a swamp.
Light Cultivation in full sun is ideal if the plant is kept outdoors, but this is not possible for greenhouse cultivation, or under plastic, because of the heat build-up, which would scorch the plant.
Temperature This should be between 15° and 24°C in winter and between 18° and 35°C in summer. The plant should never be subjected to frost.
Rest *D. spathulata* grows continuallly throughout the year, but its growth is slowed in autumn by the reduction in day length and the drop in temperature. A rest period is essential for good growth and flowering.

Pests and diseases

Guard against *Botrytis*. (See p.28.)

Varieties and closely related species

Drosera spathulata; the plant is a rosette, consisting of spatula-shaped, prostrate leaves. The glandular tentacles, which catch the prey, are easily visible, especially those on the periphery of the leaves; × 3.

D. spathulata var. *Kansai* is a native of Japan (Kansai and Chabu regions). The petiole is half as long as the limb, which is spoon-shaped, almost semi-circular, with red tentacles. The plant forms a rosette 1½in (4cm) in diameter. The flower stalk, 5-10in (12-25cm) high, carries two to twelve pink flowers, ¼in (6mm) in diameter. *D. spathulata* var. *Kanto* comes from Australia and Japan (Kanto district). The leaf blade is a continuation of the petiole, widening gradually into a club shape and rounded at the end. The tentacles are red. The leaf rosette is 1¼in (3cm) in diameter. The flower stalks, 5-8in (12-20cm) in height, carry two to sixteen flowers, ¼in (6mm) in diameter. *D. spathulata* var. *New Zealand* is a plant close to the *Kansai* variety but with wider and more rounded leaves. The rosette is 1¼in (3cm) in diameter and the flowers, ¼in (6mm) in diameter, are white. (See also p.138 for the list of *Drosera* species from temperate climates, as well as those from tropical climates.)

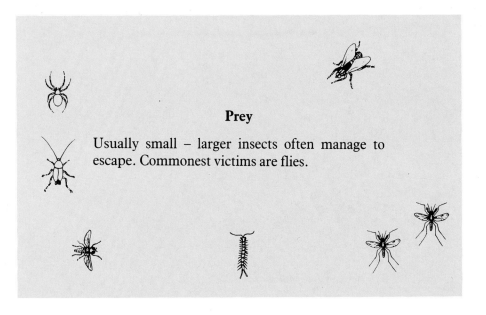

Prey

Usually small – larger insects often manage to escape. Commonest victims are flies.

Active fly-paper trap

Drosera peltata

Family Droseraceae.
Genus The genus *Drosera* comprises more than 100 species.
Origin Southwest Australia (between the towns of Hyden, Coolgardie and Norseman).

	Size	6-8in (15-20cm)
	Exposure	*half shade*
	Cultivation	*in pots*
	Humidity	*variable*
	Temperature	*4° to 30°C*
	Flowers	*winter or summer*
	Life span	*indefinite*

Etymology

The specific name of this plant is a reminder that the leaves are peltate – in other words, the petiole is attached to the middle of the limb.

Habitat

In its natural state, *Drosera peltata* lives on marshy soils, in areas surrounded by rocks. Climatically, the plant has to endure very hot and dry summers, during which it rests.

Description

Dimensions The plant is 6-8in (15-20cm) in height. The leaves are of two types. Those that form the rosette have a blade ⅛ × 5⁄16 in (4 × 8mm) and a petiole ½in (12mm) in length. The leaves on the stem measure ⅛ × ⅛in (3 × 4mm); they are carried on a petiole ⅜in (10mm) long.
Morphology The leaves at the base of the plant form a rosette, at the centre of which grows a stem, bearing alternate leaves, sometimes grouped in threes. The leaves of the rosette are elliptical and slightly concave. *D. peltata* is a tuberous plant, in other words it has a swollen underground stem. About 5⁄16in

(8mm) in diameter in the adult plant, this is red and covered in a thin, black membrane. A stolon 2¼in (6cm) long connects the bulb to the parts above ground.
Character The leaves and glandular tentacles are capable of slow movement. The leaves of the rosette are supplied with small tentacles. The other leaves, those on the stem, bear tentacles that are longer at the edge of the leaf blades than at their centres.
Flowers Inflorescences develop at the top of the main stem. They are on stalks, with each inflorescence comprising two to ten flowers. The sepals have glandular hairs and the petals are coloured from white to pink.
Ornamental effect The main ornamen-

tal feature of this plant is its long stem.
Life span Indefinite. The bulb allows the plant to survive through the long dry Australian summer.

Reproduction

Sexual reproduction Reproduction by seeds is possible. They are produced at the beginning of summer. After allowing them a respite over the summer, sow them in trays containing sieved and very wet peat. As soon as the seedlings become a little crowded, they can be thinned out.
Asexual reproduction From leaf cuttings: take off whole leaves, complete with the entire petiole. After having immersed them in a fungicide solution, plant them in very wet peat or sphagnum. As soon as the young plants begin to develop, treat them in the same way as the adult plants.

From secondary bulbs: adult plants produce lateral stolons from the original bulbs and these form new bulbs. The newest ones can be separated when repotting, which must be done before growth begins again. Each one will develop into a new plant.

Drosera peltata viewed from above, showing a flower and some leaves armed with tentacles; × 2.5.

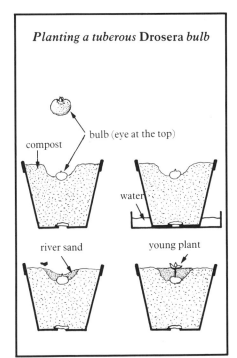

Planting a tuberous **Drosera** *bulb*

bulb (eye at the top)

compost

water

river sand

young plant

When potting, the bulb must be placed at a depth of about 2in (5cm) (after Slack 1986).

Cultivation

Compost Use peat or sphagnum; it is beneficial to add 50 per cent river sand. However, pure peat can be used as long as it is kept completely dry for six months, which corresponds to the plant's rest period. The pH must be maintained between 4.5 and 6. The pot used must be quite deep, since the bulb is planted at a depth of 2in (5cm). The eye of the bulb must be uppermost.

Watering It is advisable to keep the compost very moist during the growing period; to do this, place the pot in a bath of water ½-1¼in (1-3cm) deep. In spring, gradually reduce the wetness of the compost, which should be kept dry during summer (See 'Rest').

Light A naturally filtered light, composed of 40 to 60 per cent sunlight, is adequate for cultivating *D. peltata*. In artificial light, keep a light intensity of 10,000 to 12,000lx for eight to ten hours per day.

Temperature This must be between 4° and 25°C during the growing period and between 18° and 30°C during the rest period. *D. peltata* must not be subjected to frost.

Rest It is essential to respect the growth cycle of all *Drosera* – as six months of growth and six months of rest. Every year the bulb must store up sufficient nourishment during the growth period

to allow the plant to grow again after its summer rest. The times of the rest and growth periods can vary. Bulbs from Australia develop in spring (which corresponds to the start of the southern winter), but the timing of the start of growth can be gradually shifted so as to match the seasons of the northern hemisphere. Reproducing the plant from seeds or from cuttings allows the cycle to be regulated and both methods of propagation are perfectly possible. Plants that develop in summer receive more light and have more insects to capture.

Pests and diseases

The only insects that have been observed to attack the plant are aphids, but it should be guarded also against probable attack by microscopic fungus. (For treatment see p.28.)

Related species

D. andersoniana and *D. auriculata* are very similiar. They too are natives of Australia and *D. auriculata* is also found in New Zealand. (See p.139 for the list of species of tuberous *Drosera*.)

Despite its frail bearing, *Drosera peltata* can catch relatively large prey; × 0.9.

Prey

Prey caught is usually the size of midges, but the long tentacles on the edges of all the leaves except those at the basal rosette sometimes allow insects quite large in relation to the size of the plant to be captured.

Drosera pygmaea

Pygmy sundew

Family Droseraceae.
Genus The genus *Drosera* comprises more than 100 species.
Common names Pygmy sundew.
Origin Western Australia.

Size		3/8-3/4in (10-20mm) in diameter
Exposure		shade or half shade
Cultivation		in pots
Humidity		variable
Temperature		3° to 40°C
Flowers		summer
Life span		indefinite

Etymology

The specific name recognizes the plant's extremely small size.

Habitat

Drosera pygmaea grows naturally in marshy, constantly damp soils and in the shade of the surrounding vegetation, which filters the light. The climate of its native regions has dry, hot summers, with temperatures of between 18° and 40°C. On the other hand, winters are very rainy and this time is the active period for the plant; temperatures then vary between 3° and 22°C, with an occasional light morning frost.

Description

Dimensions. *D. pygmaea* is one of smallest species in the genus. The leaves comprise a petiole, 1/8-1/4in (4-7mm) long, and a spherical blade of about 1/16 in (2mm) diameter. The flower stalks measure no more than 1/2in (12mm).
Morphology *D. pygmaea* bears pretty white flowers in rosette formation. The upper part of their petiole is flattened. The young leaves are erect but become prostrate with age. At the beginning of the rest season, gemmae, or buds,

appear at their base: these are masses of cells that give birth to new plants.
Character The leaf blade bears glandular tentacles that capture the prey; the longest of these, around the perimeter, reach 1/16in (2mm).
Flowers The flowers are white, solitary, and are about 1/16in (2.5mm) in diameter. They are carried on stalks as fine as hair.
Ornamental effect It is principally their miniature appearance that makes them sought-after plants.
Life span Indefinite. Moreover, the species is easily reproduced via the gemmae.

Reproduction

Sexual reproduction The flowers are so frail that artificial pollination is very difficult and must be performed with the aid of a magnifying glass. But the species is autogamous and, in theory, can fertilize itself.
Asexual reproduction The most practical procedure for reproducing all the pygmy varieties of *Drosera*, and *D. pygmaea* in particular, is to use the gemmae – small spherical or flattish structures situated at the base of the leaves, which form when the temperature and the length of the photo-period diminish.

To lift them out, tilt the pot over a sheet of paper and loosen the gemmae with a small brush or a matchstick sharpened to a point. Propagate by spreading them out immediately on the surface of a seed tray filled with fine peat or sphagnum, which must be kept damp.

Gemmae, asexual reproductive organs, in the centre of a rosette of *Drosera pygmaea*: × 6.

Hybridization

No hybridization has yet been registered.

Cultivation

Compost Peat or chopped sphagnum is best; up to 50 per cent river sand or perlite may be added. Note that the pygmy *Drosera* develop a large root system, hence the need to use pots about 4in (10cm) deep.

Watering Keep the compost very damp during the growing period, but without allowing it to become flooded. The best method is to place the bottom of the pot into a shallow container of water.

Light *D. pygmaea* must be kept in filtered sunlight or in shade. In artificial light, about 10,000lx should be supplied for fourteen hours per day.

Temperature The temperature must not exceed 40°C in summer. Ambient temperatures must also not drop below 12°C in winter if continuous growth at this time is required.

Rest To imitate natural conditions, water less as soon as growth shows signs of stopping and keep the conditions dry, but not completely dehydrated, through the winter; the plant then turns into a central bud that gains some moisture from the very long and deep roots. Nevertheless, if the plant is kept damp and at a temperature above 15°C, continuous growth can be achieved over several years.

Drosera 'Lake Badgerup'; the flowers on the ends of their slender stalks; × 4.

Pests and diseases

Watch out for aphids and for mildew, a microscopic fungus.

Related species

See p.139 for the list of species of pygmy or miniature *Drosera*.

Aphids on *Drosera* 'Lake Badgerup' × 6.

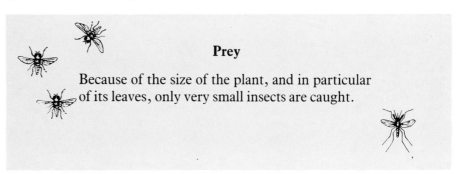

Prey

Because of the size of the plant, and in particular of its leaves, only very small insects are caught.

Pinguicula vulgaris

Active fly-paper trap

Common butterwort

Family Lentibulariaceae.
Genus The genus *Pinguicula* comprises more than 50 species.
Common name Common butterwort; French, *Grassette vulgaire;* German, *Gemeines Fettkraut.*
Origin Europe, Siberia, Canada, United States (west Pacific coast to east Carolina).

Size		2-6in (5-15cm) in diameter
Exposure		shade
Cultivation		in pots
Humidity		variable
Temperature		−1° to 20°C
Flowers		summer
Life span		indefinite

Etymology

The fact that the plant is very common and widespread has earned it its specific epithet *vulgaris.*

Habitat

Pinguicula vulgaris can be found in a variety of damp places – swamps, damp or flooded fields, rocks, peat bogs, areas of sphagnum moss, the sandy edges of rivers, etc. The pH of these places can vary a lot, from acid, through neutral, even to alkaline.

Description

Dimensions The plant, whose leaves are set in a rosette, is 2-6in (5-15cm) in diameter and 2-5in (5-12cm) high. The flower stalks 4-6in (10-15cm) high, rise from the very short main stem.
Morphology The leaves, averaging six per plant, lie flat along the ground; they are oblong and their edges fold upwards slightly. Pale green or yellowish in colour, they are thick and shiny as if coated in oil. In winter, *P. vulgaris* changes into a hibernaculum.
Character The naturally curved leaves fold gradually over prey. At first, the insects are attracted by the plant's

A flower of *Pinguicula vulgaris.* Note the spur (left) and the labellum (right); × 2.

nectar, which gives off a mushroom-like odour, and by the shiny appearance of the glands situated on the extremity of the tentacles. These glands are also responsible for catching prey; other, sessile, glands allow the victims to be digested.
Flowers Each flower stalk ends with a single violet or bluish flower, slightly tinted with white and sloping gently downwards. The corolla comprises a cylindrical spur, shaped like a trumpet, pointed at one end and bearing the floral parts at its opening. These comprise three petals joined at their base and forming the labellum, or lower lip. Two other petals, also joined at their base but pointing upwards, form the upper lip.

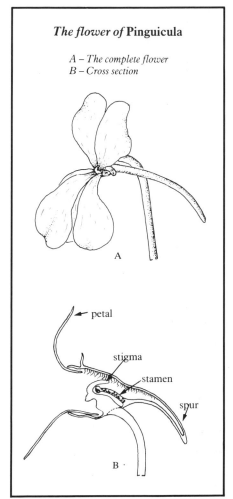

The flower of Pinguicula

A – The complete flower
B – Cross section

A

petal

stigma

stamen

spur

B

A common butterwort bearing several flower stalks; × 1.3.

There are hairs on the inside of the lower lip; their numbers increase towards the entrance of the corolla and they completely cover the outside edge, forming the palate. The stamens and the pistil are hidden deep at the back of the palate, making access difficult – any visiting insect is obliged to go right into the corolla, depositing some of the pollen it has already collected from another flower, so favouring cross-pollination.

Ornamental effect *P. vulgaris* is a very interesting plant to observe because of its method of capturing prey. In natural conditions, especially in the mountains, the flowers, which remind one a little of violets, are very attractive.

Life span *P. vulgaris* is perennial.

Reproduction

Sexual reproduction Pollinating the flowers gives fertile seeds. Cross-fertilization, between two flowers of different plants, gives the best results. Take the ripe pollen from one plant with the pointed end of a matchstick or with a fine brush, and place it on the stigma of a flower from another, which will become the mother plant. The operation is easier if the corolla is cut beforehand. The capsules ripen in about one month. Collect the seeds on a piece of paper and leave them to dry for three or four days. Then place them in small plastic bags, put them in the refrigerator, and keep them at between 0° and 3°C until spring. To sow them, spread them on the surface of seed trays filled with fine, sieved, and very damp peat. Then spray on a fungicide solution. As soon as the small plants develop, they are pricked out into seed trays filled with fine peat. *Pinguicula* raised in this way flower for the first time after two or three years.

Asexual reproduction From leaf cuttings: do this by taking off whole leaves, the oldest ones, from the mother plant. After immersing them for ten minutes in a fungicide solution, push the base of the leaves into chopped sphagnum moss or peat in the ready-prepared trays, position them in the way they normally grow – i.e. almost flat. Then keep them damp. The amount of humidity can be increased by covering them with a sheet of glass or plastic. Glass must be turned over each day in order to get rid of the droplets of condensation. The sheet of plastic can be set at an angle, using a central prop, to make a roof with near-vertical sides so that condensation runs

Active fly-paper trap
Pinguicula vulgaris

Common butterwort

Some *Pinguicula vulgaris* plants growing naturally in the French Pyrenees. The species is widespread over all the northern hemisphere but is found only in damp places – in marshes, on mossy rocks, etc. The plant spends winter in the form of a hibernaculum, a kind of compact bud, which enables it to withstand low temperatures or even frost. In summer beautiful violet flowers develop and attract insects.

off to the outside of the tray. It is best to put the cuttings in a light place and at a temperature of between 18° and 25°C. In-vitro leaf cuttings can also be made. This method uses leaf fragments, carefully cut and disinfected, and has to be carried out under sterile conditions. The seedlings obtained can then be subdivided to give many others and, when they have rooted, can be transplanted into seed trays of peat or sphagnum.

From gemmae: the gemmae are reproductive organs that develop at the base of the hibernaculum in which the plant spends the winter. They are very small structures. They can be removed using a stylet or a matchstick cut to a point, which can be dipped in water so that the gemmae adheres to it; they are then simply planted in peat. The gemmae can also be cultivated in vitro.

Hybridization

Hybridization with different species is possible, but no hybrid has yet been grown commercially.

Cultivation

Compost *P. vulgaris* grows just as well on an acid soil as on an alkaline one. A suitable acid compost can be made up of sphagnum moss or peat or a mixture of the two. Up to one third river sand, perlite or vermiculite may be added. If necessary, the acidity can be lowered by adding 15 to 20 cm^3 of dolomite (chalk powder) per litre of compost. Repot when growth returns, before the development of new roots. Choose a pot wide enough to contain the plant's rosette of leaves when fully developed, in summer. A plastic pot is perfectly suitable.

Watering The compost should be kept quite wet during the growth period. This can be achieved by immersion: put the pots in about ½in (1cm) of water. It can be renewed as soon as the level is too low or the compost can be allowed to dehydrate slightly before watering again, in order to avoid it decomposing: nevertheless, the cultivation medium must never become flooded. Watering should be reduced in autumn and the compost kept only slightly damp during the winter. The water must be as pure as possible, rainwater being the best. One can also water by misting. If this is done in the morning, it causes a slight lowering in temperature, which suits this cool, temperate-climate species.

Light Species of the *Pinguicula* genus, and *P. vulgaris* in particular, are plants that naturally live in shade, so they should be cultivated under conditions giving the equivalent of only 20 per cent of sunlight. In artificial light, supply an intensity of 10,000lx for fourteen to sixteen hours per day. The hibernaculum needs no light at all.

Temperature *P. vulgaris*, being a temperate-climate species, must be grown in moderate temperatures – between 16° and 20°C during the day and between 8° and 15°C at night. It is essential to ensure that there is a distinct difference in temperature between day and night.

Rest Rest is of vital importance for the life cycle of temperate-climate butterworts, especially *P. vulgaris*. These species must undergo a drop in temperature in order to form the hibernaculum. Failure to conform to these conditions, which set the transformation in motion, will mean the death of the plant. In the mountains, the hibernaculum is normally protected from severe cold by a layer of snow, though some plants clinging to rocks not covered by snow survive unscathed in temperatures as low as −20°C. When propagating, keep the hibernaculum in a refrigerator, not a freezer, which would be too cold for them. The usual method of conservation is as follows. When the winter buds are well formed and looking like large buds, spray them with a fungicide or soak them in a fungicide solution for at least ten minutes. Then wrap them in a small amount of slightly damp sphagnum moss and lay them out in plastic bags. Place them all in the coldest part of the refrigerator (between 1 and 4°C) for the whole of the rest period, which is six to eight months for *P. vulgaris*.

Pests and diseases

P. vulgaris may be attacked by slugs, snails, aphids and caterpillars, as well as by fungi. (For treatment see pp.28–31.)

Related species

See p.139 for the list of *Pinguicula* species from temperate climates.

Uses

Ancient medicine attributed fortifying properties to *P. vulgaris*. The species

The leaves of *Pinguicula vulgaris* are covered with small glandular tentacles, which give the plant a sheen. They are able partially to fold over captured prey (here a small butterfly).

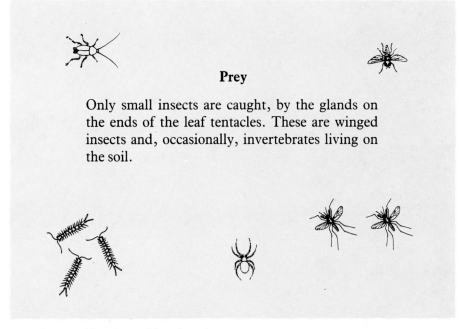

Prey

Only small insects are caught, by the glands on the ends of the leaf tentacles. These are winged insects and, occasionally, invertebrates living on the soil.

was also considered capable of curing wounds. The plant was also supposed to be purgative. Its most widespread application, even today, is in the preparation of curdled milk and its derivatives, using the leaves or their extracts, which are known for their acid properties.

Active fly-paper trap

Pinguicula caudata

Tailed butterwort

Family Lentibulariaceae.
Genus The genus *Pinguicula* comprises more than 50 species.
Common name Tailed butterwort; French, *Grassette à long éperon* or *grassette à longue queue*.
Origin Mexico.

	Size	‘4-8in (10-20cm) in diameter
	Exposure	*shade*
	Cultivation	*in pots*
	Humidity	*moderate*
	Temperature	*3° to 30°C*
	Flowers	*summer and winter*
	Life span	*several years*

Pinguicula moranensis flower seen in profile. The 'spur' is particularly long in this form – *P.m. caudata* × 1.2.

History and etymology

What is now known to be one of several forms of the species *Pinguicula moranensis*, but was originally thought to be a distinct species, *P. caudata*, was described in 1832 by the German botanist D.F.L. Schlechtendhal, from samples collected by the traveller G. Schiede near a place in Mexico named Cuesta Grande de Chiconquiaco. The name *caudata* comes from the Latin *caudatus*, meaning 'ending in a tail'. It refers to the spur, a kind of cylinder formed by the joining of the bases of the three lower petals, which is particularly well developed in the flowers of *P. moranensis caudata* – it reaches a length of 1½-2in (4-5cm).

Habitat

In its original site in Mexico, *P. moranensis* grows in large, damp, peaty woods, on a variety of soils, acid, neutral, or alkaline. It can withstand short periods of drought.

Description

Dimensions During the growing period, the leaves reach 4in (10cm) in length and 2¼in (6cm) in width, and the flower stalks are 4-8in (10-20cm) high.

Morphology *P. moranensis* is a heterophyllous species – the plant's summer form is different from its winter one, the changes concerning mainly the leaves.

Summer form: set in a rosette, the leaves hug the ground. Either with or without a petiole, they are oblong and fleshy.

Winter form: the hemispherical rosette is composed of more numerous and smaller leaves than the summer form, they are also more tightly packed and end in a point.

Character *P. moranensis* differs from other species of the genus (*P. vulgaris*, for example), in that its leaves hardly roll over at all in contact with a potential prey. Indeed, the leaves of the winter form have no movement at all. On the other hand, all the leaves have both sessile glands (which digest prey) and stalked glands (which capture it).

Flowers The flower stalks, like the leaves, are pale green in colour. Each stalk bears a single flower which, in the summer form, is 2in (5cm) long and 1½in (4cm) wide. Flower colour is variable, going from white to purple, but usually it is pale or deep pink. The three lower petals, joined together, form a tube ending in a narrow and very long 'spur'. The flowers of the winter form are slightly smaller than those of the summer form.

82

Ornamental effect The plant is interesting because of the particularly large leaves of the summer form and because of its large and profuse flowers.
Life span Several years.

Reproduction

Sexual reproduction For good results, it is best to cross-pollinate: using a fine brush take the pollen from one plant and deposit it on the stigma of another. After about a month, the seeds will be ready for collection. Sow them in spring on seed trays of fine, damp peat and thin them out as the plants develop. They will not flower for two or three years.
Asexual reproduction Cuttings should be taken, preferably in February, from the small, winter leaves, which should be set out on chopped sphagnum moss. After a few weeks, small buds appear, develop roots and leaves, and become young plantlets.

Hybridization

P. × *scthos*, from *P. ehrlesai* and *P. moranensis*, is now available commercially.

Cultivation

Compost *P. moranensis* is happy on either an acid or alkaline soil. Sphagnum moss or peat can be used, mixed or on their own. The acidity can be reduced by adding dolomite. (See *Pinguicula vulgaris*: 'Compost'.)
Watering Keep the compost damp in summer, without over-watering. Water less in winter.
Light Although *P. moranensis* is a warm-climate plant, always avoid exposure to direct sunlight. In artificial light, the intensity needs to be roughly 10,000lx.
Temperature During the growing period, temperature must be between 18° and 30°C. It is best to observe a difference of a few degrees between day and night. Protect the plant from frost in winter and if possible keep it at between 3° and 10°C.
Rest Although it slows down, growth continues in winter. Therefore, the plant must still receive light as well as sufficient aeration. Monthly spraying with a fungicide will reduce the risk of rot and fungi during this time.

A fine example of *Pinguicula moranensis caudata*, displaying four flower stalks; × 0.5.

Pests and disease

Be especially aware of fungi during cultivation and also of possible attack by slugs, snails, caterpillars, or aphids. (For treatment see pp.28–31.)

Related species

See p.139 for the list of species of *Pinguicula* from warm or semi-tropical climates.

Prey
The most common prey is midges and other insects of similar size.

Active fly-paper trap

Pinguicula lutea

Yellow butterwort

Family Lentibulariaceae.
Genus The genus *Pinguicula* comprises more than 50 species.
Common names Yellow butterwort; French *Grassette jaune*.
Origin Coastal plains and hinterland of the southwestern United States, from South Carolina, through Florida, to Louisiana.

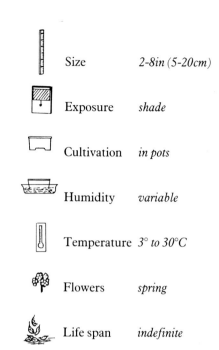

Size	*2-8in (5-20cm)*
Exposure	*shade*
Cultivation	*in pots*
Humidity	*variable*
Temperature	*3° to 30°C*
Flowers	*spring*
Life span	*indefinite*

History and etymology

Pinguicula lutea was introduced into England in 1816. The specific name reflects the colour of the flowers – *lutea* means yellow in Latin.

Habitat

This plant grows around pine trees on poor, often sandy soils or, by contrast, on open, damp, even swampy, land where it is protected from the sun by the surrounding grasses and vegetation.

Description

Dimensions The length of the leaves varies between ¾in (2cm) and 3in (8cm). The flower stalks are 2-8in (5-20cm) high.
Morphology The radical leaves are set in a rosette. They are pale green and roughly oval in shape. The edges of the limb are well rolled over and make the ends of the leaves look quite pointed. *P. lutea*, like *P. moranensis*, has winter leaves of reduced size.
Character Rolling up the leaf edges enables the plant to increase the amount of contact between captured insects and the ciliate glands on the surface of the leaves. The sessile glands, which have a much simpler structure than the ciliate glands, digest the prey.
Flowers Each spindly flower stalk bears one flower. It is formed of a green calyx, covered with grey hair, and a deep chrome-yellow corolla, ¾-1⅜in (2-3.5cm) in diameter. The three lower petals form a spur, a kind of gently curved tube, ⅜-⅝in (1-1.5cm) long. In its original sites, the flowering season extends from February to May.
Ornamental effect The ornamental interest of *P. lutea* resides in its flowers, relatively large and magnificently coloured.
Life span *P. lutea* is a perennial plant with an indefinite life span.

Reproduction

Sexual reproduction As for other species of *Pinguicula*, it is best, if possible, to cross-fertilize. The pollen from one flower is deposited on the stigma of another, which will produce the seeds. When they mature, approximately one month after fertilization, they are lifted out and put to dry. They should then be placed in a refrigerator before being sown in spring in seedbeds of sieved, damp peat.
Asexual reproduction During the rest period, take off the number of leaves required and soak them for a few minutes in a fungicide solution. Then set them out on chopped sphagnum moss or peat, just as they would lie when growing naturally. Keep the medium quite wet and, if necessary, place a sheet of glass or plastic over the seed tray, taking care that the condensation does not fall on the seedlings.

Hybridization

There is no known hybrid of these species.

Cultivation

Compost *P. lutea* is a plant from acid soil, with a pH of between 5 and 6. Either peat or sphagnum can be used for compost, to which one third river sand, perlite, or vermiculite may be added.
Watering The compost must be kept moist during the growing period.
Light Exposure to full sunlight is not recommended. In artificial light, take care not to exceed an intensity of 10,000lx.
Temperature Temperatures can vary between 3° and 10°C during the rest period and between 18° and 30°C during the growth period.
Rest Growth stops during the winter. The small leaves of the winter form

The first flower of a young *Pinguicula lutea*. The name of the species comes from the colour of its flowers. Various insects (midges and whitefly) are trapped by its leaves; × 3.5.

develop very little. To avoid rot or fungus, spray the plants with a fungicide in autumn and repeat this operation each month during the rest period. The amount of light can also be reduced.

Pests and diseases

P. lutea can be attacked by various insects (aphids, caterpillars), by molluscs (snails, slugs), and by fungus. (For treatment, see pp. 28–31.)

Related species

See p.139 for the list of *Pinguicula* species from warm or semi-tropical climates.

Prey

Because of the small size of its leaf tentacles, only small insects are caught, mostly flies.

85

Byblis gigantea

Passive fly-paper trap

Rainbow plant

Family Byblidaceae.
Genus The genus *Byblis* comprises two species, *B. gigantea* and *B. liniflora*.
Common names Rainbow plant; French, *Plante arc-en-ciel;* German, *Regenbogenpflanze.*
Origin *B. gigantea:* southwest Australia. *B. liniflora:* Western Australia, Queensland, and New Guinea.

Size		*12-25in (30-65cm)*
Exposure		*full sun or half shade*
Cultivation		*in pots*
Humidity		*moderate*
Temperature		*4° to 35°C*
Flowers		*end of spring to beginning of summer*
Life span		*several years*

A *Byblis liniflora* flower ready to open. Two midges have been caught on the flower stalk; × 2.5.

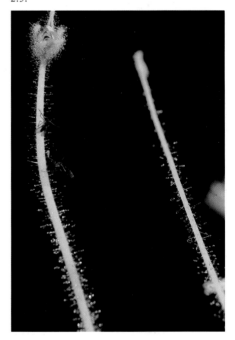

History and etymology

The *Byblis* genus, originally classified in the Pittosporaceae family, was described around 1848 by Jules-Émile Planchon and George Bentham in the review *Flora Australiensis.* About 1860, Thomas Lang connected it to the *Pinguicula* and classified it with the Lentibulariaceae. It was Karl Domin, in 1922, who classified it definitely in the Byblidaceae, along with the type species *Byblis liniflora,* sometimes cited under the name of *B. linifolia.* The flower is similiar to that of flax (genus *Linum).*

The genus name, *Byblis,* is that of the beautiful daughter of Miletos, sister of Caunos, with whom she fell in love. Because her love was not returned, she hanged herself and was changed into a fountain.

Habitat

B. gigantea is a perennial plant, found in southwest Australia, especially the Swan River region, not far from Perth, in swampy, sandy soils. In other regions, it is usually found along the banks of rivers and streams, but it also grows in drier areas, in sandy soils containing both clay and some humus. It dries up completely and loses its foliage during the hot, dry summers. Growth returns with the rains. In damp sites, the plant is green all year round. Temperatures in its natural habitat vary between 14° and 40°C, according to season.

B. liniflora is also found around water and in river beds on sandy soils, in conditions similiar to those enjoyed by *B. gigantea.* After brush fires, growth returns with the rains, from the stump or the roots. The two species are sun-loving plants, but they grow equally well in moderate shade.

Description

Dimensions *B. gigantea* looks like a shrub, 12-25in (30-65cm) high, with leaves 4-10in (10-25cm) long. *B. liniflora* is very similiar, but slightly smaller in size. The plants have a tendency to bend over and do not grow to more than 12in (30cm). The leaves are 2¼-3½in (6-9cm) long.
Morphology The underground parts comprise a very hard rhizome, which looks like wood. The main stem throws out lateral branches. The alternate, linear leaves have an almost triangular section, rounded at the apex. Yellowish green in colour, they look rather like long pieces of string.
Character The *Byblis* are passive plants; their leaves are completely covered with fixed, immobile, glandular hairs, the longest of which catch insects attracted by their shining droplets of sticky mucilage. The struggles of the victims serve only to increase the amount of mucilage produced. They finally come into contact with the tiny, sessile, digestive glands, set in lines on either side of the leaves and on the stalks. These glands are so small that they have to be examined with a microscope. They sec-

The *Byblis liniflora* flower, on the end of its stalk, covered with glandular tentacles; × 3.

A young *Byblis liniflora* beginning to flower. Some young leaves, just forming, are still rolled up into a crook. All parts of the plant are covered with glandular tentacles. This confers on the plant not only an undisputed ornamental value, but also a very effective means of catching prey; × 0.7.

rete enzymes that digest then assimilate captured prey. The plant sometimes captures so many insects that it seems to be completely covered in them.

Flowers The flower appear on the stalks that grow from the base of each leaf. In *B. gigantea* they are 1½in (4cm) in diameter, violet or pink; in *B. liniflora* they are 1¼in (3cm) in diameter, and green. They open at the sunniest times of the day and fade at the end of the afternoon. They have five sepals, five petals, and five stamens. The ovary, which has two compartments, contains many ovules. It is surmounted by a lengthened style. The fruit is a globular many-spermed capsule. The seeds are small and oblong.

Ornamental effect The drops of mucilage, seen against a good light, make a brilliant display, justifying the plant's common name of rainbow plant.

Life span It is not possible to give precise figures, but the *Byblis* certainly live for many years. Young plants grown from seeds sometimes, though, behave like annuals – they do not reappear in spring because they have not survived the cold of winter.

Passive fly-paper trap
Byblis gigantea

Rainbow plant

Reproduction

Sexual reproduction Seeds can be obtained by pollinating the flowers in the afternoon (they become too wilted by the evening): move the pollen on to the stigma with a fine brush. The capsules reach maturity in about four to six weeks. *B. liniflora* seeds should be dried and placed in plastic bags in the refrigerator for at least two months before being sown. The medium for the seed trays should be the same as for the adult plants – peat, sphagnum, river sand, and perlite. Spray or water with a fungicide or roll the seeds in a fungicide powder before sowing. Keep them slightly moist and maintain quite a high temperature, between 20° and 30°C. Note that the seeds of *B. gigantea* germinate less easily than those of *B. liniflora*. In fact, *B. gigantea*, in natural conditions, suffers brush fires and the high temperatures encourage germination. There are several possible ways of reproducing this phenomenon:

Soak the seeds in water for twenty-four hours. Then sow them on wet peat and cover them with several layers of wet paper or with paper and a wet sponge on top. Put them in an incubator (at 80° to 90°C) for one night (six to eight hours).

After sowing the seeds, soaked in water for the previous twenty-four hours, place the tray over steam for one hour.

Pour boiling water over the seeds and the wet peat four times in succession.

Asexual reproduction Stem cuttings: cut the stems at the beginning of the rest period or when growth returns. Cut the top half 2-6in (5-15cm) from the apex. Place the cuttings in sphagnum moss, keeping two thirds of each stem above the surface. Keep the cuttings damp, at temperatures of between 20° and 30°C, and give them as much light as possible. Root development can occur within three months. The mother plant continues to grow and produces a new stem.

A young shoot, one month old, cultivated in vitro. Germination occurs in fifteen days using this technique, against the two months needed with traditional methods; × 13.

Cut the stem 2in (5cm) above soil level when growth starts again.

Leaf cuttings: This technique is suitable for *B. liniflora*. Place the leaves on damp sphagnum moss in the same way as for stem cuttings.

Roof cuttings: It is possible to take as much as one third of the main root system of vigorous plants. Slice the root cutting into 1¼in (3cm) sections and place them on wet sphagnum, under a good light and at temperatures which must be between 20° and 30°C.

Hybridization

No hybridization between the two species of *Byblis*, nor any intergeneric hybridization, has been recorded.

Cultivation

Compost Sphagnum is suitable for young or adult plants. Peat can be substituted and up to two thirds river sand or perlite may be added. Fertilizers are unnecessary if the plant catches insects.

Watering The compost must always be kept wet during the growth period, but do not flood it.

Light *B. gigantea*: outdoor cultivation must be in full sunlight. In artificial light, maintain an intensity of 12,000lx for fourteen to sixteen hours per day, depending on time of year.

B. liniflora: outdoors, light shade is needed. Artificial light requirements are the same as for *B. gigantea*.

Temperature For constant growth, the temperature must stay above 18°C but never rise above 35°C. The optimum temperatures are 21°C for *B. gigantea* and 18°C for *B. liniflora*.

Rest Plants subjected to temperatures lower than 18°C in winter go into their rest period. It is then necessary to keep them from frost, above 4°C. Water less, just enough to keep the compost slightly damp. Finally, in artificial light, give about nine hours of light per day, at 8,000lx.

Size If the plants grow too much or to an awkward size, the stems will need to be cut back to 2-4in (5-10cm) above the soil at the start of the growth period. New shoots grow from the base and the plant assumes the shape of a compact tuft. The trimmings can be used as cuttings (see 'Asexual reproduction').

Pests and diseases

Lack of light and excess humidity can encourage the development of fungi. Harmful insects do not seem to thrive on *Byblis*.

Plate from '*Curtis's Botanical Magazine*' (1902), showing *Byblis gigantea* and its various parts.

Prey

Prey is exclusively insects, of which a very varied assortment is caught. Because most of the leaves are covered with glandular hairs, catches are made in great numbers all over the plant, which at times may be completely covered.

Drosophyllum lusitanicum

Passive fly-paper trap

Portuguese sundew

Family Droseraceae.
Genus The genus *Drosophyllum* contains only one species, *D. lusitanicum.*
Common names Portuguese sundew; French, *Drosophylle;* German, *Taublatt.*
Origin Portugal, Spain and Morocco.

Size		*up to 5ft (1.5m)*
Exposure		*full sun*
Cultivation		*in pots*
Humidity		*moderate*
Temperature		*3° to 40°C*
Flowers		*spring*
Life span		*indefinite*

History and etymology

Samples from the botanical gardens at Coimbra in Portugal were sent to Kew Gardens, England, in 1869 and at round about the same time, some plants from the coastal regions of Morocco were sent to Charles Darwin. But the plant was before then being used to catch flies – its local name in Portugal means fly swallower.

The generic name comes from *drosos*, 'dew', and *phyllon*, 'leaf'.

Habitat

In natural conditions, *Drosophyllum lusitanicum* grows in poor, rocky, or sandy ground, on hillsides or at the edges of the sea. In summer, the species has to suffer long periods of drought, during which the only water it receives is a nightly dew. It is the only member of the Droseraceae family to live in such dry regions.

Description

Dimensions Older plants form shrubs with woody branches ⅝in (1.5cm) in diameter. They can reach 5ft (1.5cm) in height, although the branches bend under their own weight. The leaves are 4-8in (10-22cm) long by ⅛in (3mm) wide. The flower stalks are 12in (30cm) high.

Morphology There are numerous leaves on the ends of the stems. Underneath, the older, dehydrated leaves surround the stems, which they partly hide. The leaf is linear and terminates in a point. When young it looks like a scroll, rolled up outwards like the leaves of *Byblis* species. Otherwise, the edges are rolled inwards; the under-surface is convex and the upper surface concave, forming a narrow channel in the middle.

Character *D. lusitanicum* is a passive plant whose leaves are furnished with two kinds of glands – tentacle glands under and along the edges of the leaves and sessile glands, distributed over almost the whole surface of the leaf. The tentacle glands, which are immobile, secrete a mucilage that sticks to any insect it contacts. The prey struggles and so slips down towards the lower tentacles, which quickly cover it with mucilage; it then dies by suffocation. Then it comes into contact with the transparent sessile glands, which secrete the enzymes and acids necessary for digestion. The tentacle glands are capable of rapidly producing more mucilage for capture. There are also tentacle glands on the stalks, the bracts, and the sepals, but they are not linked to any digestive glands.

Flowers Yellow, and measuring 1¼-1½in (3-4cm) in diameter, the flowers are set in an umbel on stalks with bracts. Each flower bears five sharp oblong sepals and five spooned, bright yellow petals; the stamens, numbering anything between ten and thirty are inserted under the ovary and have short yellow anthers. The flowers have the unusual characteristic of opening during the day and closing at night. The ovary is oblong and the egg-shaped fruit, ¾in (18mm) long, is smooth and tough. It produces many hard seeds, held within a central receptacle.

Ornamental effect The plant is special because of its shiny foliage, from which the glossy red tentacles stick out; the flowers are attractive but short-lived.

Life span *D. lusitanicum* is a perennial species, but it is not an easy subject for cultivation.

Reproduction

Sexual reproduction 'Strong' plants have flowers that self-fertilize – in other words they produce fertile seeds by fertilizing with their own pollen. Germination can sometimes take three or four years because of the integument (or outer wall), which is very hard. To speed up germination, pierce the shell or slice off a small section of the face, to reveal the inside, white in colour. This method allows germination to take place in only four to five weeks. Sow at the end of summer on ready-prepared composts or on a mixture of one third sphagnum and two thirds river sand or perlite. When sowing, space the seeds out and cover them with a layer of

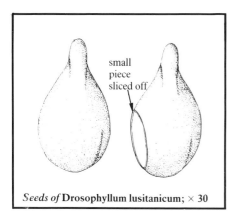

small piece sliced off

Seeds of **Drosophyllum lusitanicum**; × 30

compost as thick as their own diameter. Treat with fungicide and keep the compost damp until the seeds germinate, in temperatures of between 16° and 25°C. From the moment when the plants appear, keep the compost almost continually dry. Transplant the shoots with as much of their roots as possible so as not to damage them. Only one plant per pot must be cultivated or growth will suffer.

Asexual reproduction It is possible to reproduce *D. lusitanicum* from cuttings.

Hybridization

No case of hybridization has yet been reported.

Cultivation

Compost Among the various possible mixtures of compost, the most appropriate is one quarter sphagnum and three quarters river sand. In general, sphagnum and peat form the basis of cultivation mediums. Ten ml of dolomite per litre of compost can be added in order to imitate conditions in the original sites, which are often alkaline.

Watering Never soak the compost. Keep it wet but not too wet in winter and respect the dry season by giving very little water. Regular watering may allow two successive years of growth.

Light *D. lusitanicum* likes full sun and must be exposed as much as possible to

the light, except under greenhouse glass where it would become too hot. In weak light, the tentacles stay green and the plant withers.

Temperature. *D. lusitanicum* lives in temperatures of between 3° and 40°C, but the best results are obtained between 10° and 28°C. The plant can withstand hoar frosts.

Rest A rest period is necessary to replicate natural conditions, so water very sparsely during summer.

Pests and diseases

Aphids, mealy bugs, and scale insects can attack the plants, which may also suffer from botrytis or rot. (For treatment, see pp. 28–9.)

Flowers of *Drosophyllum lusitanicum* at different stages of development; × 1.

Prey

Prey, attracted by mucilage that smells like honey, is usually small flying insects such as mosquitoes, midges, and small flies.

91

Passive pitfall trap

Darlingtonia californica

Cobra lily

Family Sarraceniaceae.
Genus The genus *Darlingtonia* contains only one species, *D. californica*.
Common names Cobra lily, cobra plant, California pitcher plant; French, *Plante cobra*.
Origin United States (the Rocky Mountains, from Oregon to northern California, up to 9000ft (2800m) altitude).

Size	up to 32in (80cm)
Exposure	half shade
Cultivation	in pots or a terrarium
Humidity	high
Temperature	15° to 22°C
Flowers	spring
Life span	indefinite

History and etymology

The species was discovered in 1841 near Mount Shasta, California, and described in 1853. The generic name recognizes an American botanist, Dr William Darlington, of Winchester, Pennsylvania.

Habitat

The plant grows in sphagnum moss or acid humus, up to an altitude of 9000ft (2800m); examples of the species found at lower altitudes grow along water courses formed by melting snow, where the roots can be maintained at cool temperatures.

Description

Dimensions Young plants grow to no more than 2in (5cm) in the first year of cultivation. Adult plants can reach 32in (80cm) and the flower stalks sometimes 3ft (1m).
Morphology *Darlingtonia californica* is a plant with a short, thick rhizome. The fibrous roots are brownish-black. The radical leaves (growing directly from the rhizome) consist of pitchers in a rosette around the rhizome. They are either erect or slightly upturned, of greatly varying size. Narrow at the base,

Upper part of the ascidium of *Darlingtonia californica*, showing the double appendage on which insects can land, as well as the entrance or mouth; × 0.8.

The entrance of a pitcher. When viewed against the light, the dome appears translucent; × 1.2.

they gradually widen towards the top, which ends in a dome or hood, with the trap's orifice underneath. At the front of this hangs a double appendage, shaped like a fishtail. The pitcher, which has a wing, or narrow extension of the leaf blade, along its whole length, twists during its development through 180°, so that the opening is at the other side to

Vertical section of a *D. californica* trap; the hairs prevent prey from going back up; × 5.

the rhizome from which it grew. The pitchers are green at the base and spotted white and red towards the top; the fishtail appendage becomes very red in well-lit conditions.

Character The lure which first attracts the insect consists of the shape and the colours of the pitcher. Also, nectar is emitted by glands along the surface of the upper part of the dome. The appendages serve as a point of access for insects entering the ascidium. The whitish blotches on the dome are transparent and look like windows when viewed from the inside. These patches, containing no chlorophyll, mislead any insect venturing inside into thinking it has a means of escape. Hairs on the inner walls force the prey to descend towards the base of the urn, with no chance of ascent. The captive insect drowns in a liquid which has a bacteriological action and the plant gradually absorbs the nutritional solution thus provided. The

A *Darlingtonia californica* in flower. The flower stalk stands well above the characteristically shaped pitchers. The flower itself is also unusual – besides the five green sepals it has five brown petals, all joined to each other, forming a kind of small bell; × 1.5.

volume of the liquid inside varies according to the number of insects caught. The plant produces no enzymes.

Flowers The flower opens at the start of the growth period and is borne by a stalk higher than the foliage; there is usually only one per plant. The stalk bends over at the top in a semicircle and

Darlingtonia californica
Cobra lily

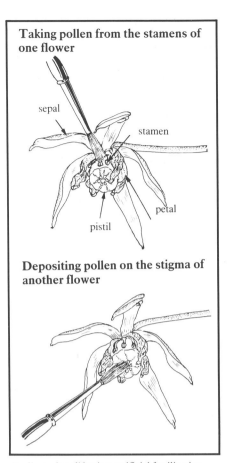

Taking pollen from the stamens of one flower

sepal

stamen

petal

pistil

Depositing pollen on the stigma of another flower

Darlingtonia californica: artificial fertilization.

The flower after removal of some of the petals; × 1.1.

the flower looks as if it is suspended. After fertilization, it adopts a vertical position, thus preventing the seeds from escaping too rapidly. The stalk has lance-like bracts. The flower, 2in (5cm) in diameter on average, is composed of five green, triangular, slender sepals and five brown, bell-shaped petals, closed tightly against each other. Each petal has a V-shaped cut on each side so that, when butted together, the corolla forms five round holes to allow pollinating insects to pass through. The ovary is pear-shaped and situated at the centre, forming a continuation of the top end of the stalk. In its lower part it has a prominent stigma, like a five-pointed star. The stamens, numbering twelve to fifteen, are fixed around the base of the ovary.

Ornamental effect *D. californica* is a curious plant because of the peculiar shape of its pitchers which has been likened to a cobra ready to pounce.

Life span The plant's life span is unlimited; *D. californica* is a hardy species whose rhizome produces new shoots and new ascidia each year.

Reproduction

Sexual reproduction The flower is made up in such a way that in natural conditions there is cross-fertilization. When the insect enters the bell formed by the petals, its wings, which carry the pollen from previously-visited flowers, make contact with the stigma. On exploring inside, the visitor loads up with pollen, but the shape of the ovary prevents it from touching the stigma when it leaves. In artificial cultivation, too, it is better to cross-fertilize, since the seeds so produced are more viable than those produced when the flower fertilizes itself. Artificial fertilization means taking the pollen from one flower using a fine brush and depositing it on the stigmas of others. In the wild, the club-headed seeds, which have tiny

needles on them, ripen in autumn and are covered in snow through the winter. To replicate this, put the seeds out to dry for a few days after they have been collected and keep them in a refrigerator or freezer through the winter. Some carnivorous-plant growers claim that the best procedure is to keep the seeds in the refrigerator for about two months, then in the freezer for another two months, and then to sow them in spring. The seeds are sown on the surface of trays or pots filled with finely sieved, damp peat. To sow, put the seeds on a piece of paper, folded down the middle, slope the paper down towards the seed tray and tap gently with a finger, letting the seeds fall slowly on to the peat and so spreading them out evenly across the compost. Then treat with fungicide. As soon as the small plants have appeared, they can undergo their first transplant on to trays filled with the same mixture, to give them enough room. Make two or three transplantations into trays or communal pots before repotting the little plants into individual pots when they reach 1½ or 2in (4-5cm) in height. Often, the seedlings are kept in trays for the first year and then picked out in their

own little jars the following spring. The young plants then go through the same winter rest period as the adult plants. From seedling to the adult plant takes five years.

Asexual reproduction Adult plants multiply by producing secondary rhizomes on the main one. Those secondary rhizomes are the start of new plants and they can be separated from the mother plant when they have enough roots. Leaf cuttings can also be taken, or a small portion of the rhizome, cut into sections, can be used for cuttings. Place the cuttings in sphagnum or peat and keep them constantly damp. Root developments can take between one and eight months.

Hybridization

There is no known hybrid of *D. californica*.

Cultivation

Compost A compost based on pure sphagnum moss is perfectly suitable.

Failing this, use peat. River sand can be added. Keep the pH at around 5 and ensure the compost is well drained. The rhizome should be placed just under the surface so that the base of the ascidium is just at the surface of the compost. Use pots that are quite large and deep to suit the eventual size of the plants.

Watering Always keep the compost very damp. The plant can withstand heat, but not the roots, which must have a supply of cold water – either rainwater or, failing this, as pure a water as possible.

Light Expose the plant to as much light as possible while still keeping the compost cool.

Temperature In the growth period, temperatures between 15° and 22°C are ideal. In the wild, the plant is subjected to light frosts in winter and temperatures of up to 38°C in summer. But if temperatures go as high as that in cultivation, the compost must be kept below 22°C by constantly supplying it with cold water.

Rest A winter rest period must be given, with at least four months at low temperatures, watering less and less but without letting the compost dry out. *Darlingtonia* are hardy plants and can withstand frost. Remove any leaves that have dried up.

Pests and diseases

The greatest enemy of *Darlingtonia* is *Oïdium*, a fungus which develops as white blotches. It is treated by spraying, or by soaking, with fungicide. If there is evidence of *Oïdium* on neighbouring plants, do not hesitate to take preventive measures. Mealy bugs and scale insects can appear, especially on the ascidium, and aphids may settle on the flower stalks.

Enlargement of the ascidium wall of a *Darlingtonia californica* attacked by *Oïdium*; this fungus develops its white filaments quickly, suffocating the cells and causing tissue death; × 18.

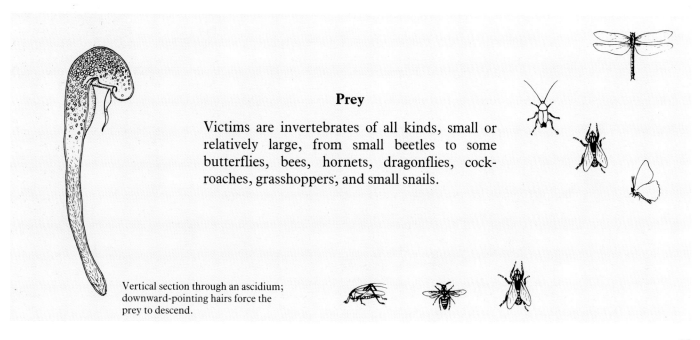

Prey

Victims are invertebrates of all kinds, small or relatively large, from small beetles to some butterflies, bees, hornets, dragonflies, cockroaches, grasshoppers, and small snails.

Vertical section through an ascidium; downward-pointing hairs force the prey to descend.

Passive pitfall trap

Heliamphora nutans

Sun pitcher plant

Family Sarraceniaceae.
Genus The genus *Heliamphora* comprises 6 species.
Common names Sun pitcher plant; French, *Héliamphore*; German, *Sumpfkrug*.
Origin Guyana, Venezuela (Mount Roraima).

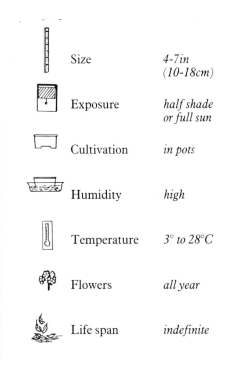

Size	4-7in (10-18cm)
Exposure	half shade or full sun
Cultivation	in pots
Humidity	high
Temperature	3° to 28°C
Flowers	all year
Life span	indefinite

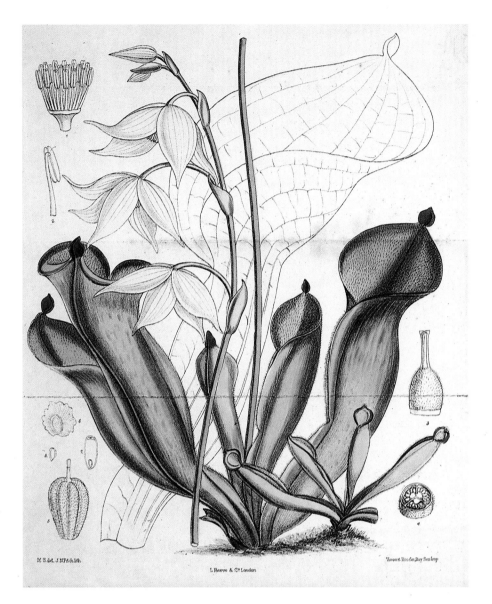

History and etymology

The *Heliamphora* genus was discovered in 1839, in marshy savanna near Mount Roraima, by Sir Robert Schomburgk, while he was surveying the borders of Guyana. The plant was described, under the name *Heliamphora nutans*, by the English botanist George Bentham in *Transactions of the London Linnean Society* in 1840. The species was re-imported by Burke in 1881 and its flowers were immortalized in plates published in Van Houtte's *Flora of Gardens and Greenhouses* and in Curtis's *Botanical Magazine*.

The generic name derives from the Greek words *hêlios*, 'sun', and *amphora*. The reference to the sun is because the first plants to be gathered were found growing in full sun; *amphora* alludes to the shape of the types of all *Heliamphora*. The name *nutans*, which means leaning in Latin, was given to the species because of the curvature of the flower stalks and the pendant nature of the flowers.

Opposite: rudimentary trumpets of *Heliamphora minor*, a species related to *Heliamphora nutans*, surmounted by a miniature operculum, or beak. Its colour and its nectar glands are an attraction for insects; × 1.2.

Habitat

Like all members of the genus, *Heliamphora nutans* is a mountain plant, growing in marshes at an average altitude of 6500ft (2000m) in a cool and very humid climate. It is exposed to very bright sunlight and lives under a perfectly clear sky.

Description

Dimensions The leaves, rolled into a trumpet shape, are 4-7in (10-18cm) high and ¾-1¼in (2-3cm) in diameter.
Morphology The leaves forming the pitchers grow directly from a rhizome. Each pitcher is narrow at the base and also constricted towards the top. It has two not very prominent, longitudinal wings, which seem to correspond to the line where the leaf edges join. On the

Plate, published in Curtis's *Botanical Magazine* in 1830, showing *Heliamphora nutans*. The stalk bears several white flowers; × 0.5.

opposite side is a large, prominent, longitudinal vein, at the top of which is a small, spoon-shaped appendage, the operculum, or lid, which has nectar-bearing glands on its inner surface. It overhangs the wide and oblique opening to the trap. Waxy or velvety in appearance, the pitchers are green, with red or purple veins.
Character The pitchers attract, catch, and digest insects. Internally they have four distinct zones. At the top, the lid attracts the prey with its red under-surface and its glands. The way the lid bends forward protects these from the rain. A little further down, the interior of the pitcher is supplied with fine, downward-pointing hairs, which prevent any prey venturing inside from

97

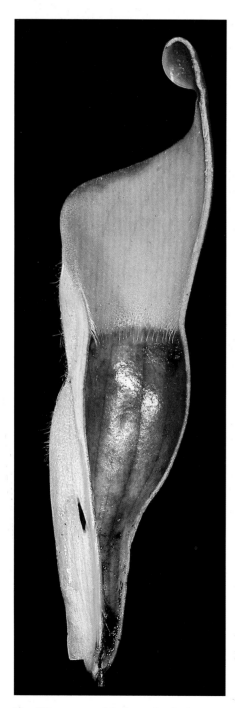

Passive pitfall trap

Heliamphora nutans

Sun pitcher plant

The different zones of the internal wall of *Heliamphora minor*; × 1.8.

retreating. This zone also has nectar glands. Further down is a smooth hairless region, on which victims can find no footing. The lower part has an inner wall lined with hairs, also preventing any escape for the prey. It contains water, full of bacteria, which dissolve prey and allow their absorption. The plant has no digestive glands.

Flowers The red-tinted flower stalks grow higher than the foliage. They are topped by two to seven pendant flowers, borne on curved stalks. There is a bract where these join the main stalk. The flowers have no petals. The central pistil has a pubescent ovary and a smooth stigma; it is surrounded by the stamens. The flowers are white and become pink with age.

Ornamental effect The plant's distinguishing feature is its flowers, which are both simple and decorative.

Life span As with every perennial plant, the life span is indefinite in good cultivation conditions.

Reproduction

Sexual reproduction The flower cannot fertilize itself; in fact, when the male cells (the pollen) are mature, the female cells, and therefore the stigma, are no longer receptive. In theory, the stigma is receptive in the week following the opening of the flower, and the pollen of the same flower can only be gathered a few days later. Each flower must therefore be fertilized, in the days following its opening, with pollen taken from another flower that has already opened. However, the pollen can be kept in the refrigerator. The seeds also are placed after collection in the refrigerator at a temperature of between 5° and 7°C; they are left there all winter. Sow them in spring on a compost of sieved peat or chopped, sieved and boiled sphagnum.

Asexual reproduction When the rhizome of vigorous plants has grown several shoots, these can be separated or the rhizome cut into small sections, as with the *Sarracenia* (See *Sarracenia purpurea*). But the *Heliamphora*, especially *H. nutans*, are more fragile and care must be taken not to damage their brittle roots. The cut sections must be treated with fungicide before placing them on the surface of the compost. It is best to do this in spring.

Hybridization

No hybridization has yet been recorded.

Cultivation

Compost Use a compost made up of sphagnum moss or of a mixture of sphagnum and peat. The plants must be repotted once per year. When doing this, place the rhizome at the surface so that it is barely covered by the compost. Remember that the roots, which are often 4-8in (10-20cm) long, are very fragile.

Watering The compost must be kept very damp in summer; to achieve this, leave the base of the pots in a bed of water. The rest of the plant must be kept damp by spraying; make sure that there is always water at the bottom of the ascidia. Do not use fertilizers, they may damage the plant.

Light The plants can be exposed to sunlight, as long as the temperature at plant level does not exceed 25° or 26°C. In artificial light, intensities of 15,000 to 18,000 lx are needed.

Temperature The intense heat of summer must be avoided. Temperatures must be maintained at between 10° and 28°C in summer and between 3° and 15°C in winter.

Rest Winter is the rest period; at this time, keep the compost just slightly damp.

Pests and diseases

Cochineals sometimes, albeit rarely, settle on *H. nutans*. Its only other enemies seem to be aphids and *Botrytis*. In all cases, avoid using copper-based insecticides, since these are harmful to the plant. (For treatment, see pp.28–9.)

Related species

The *Heliamphora* genus comprises five other species besides *H. nutans*. *H. heterodoxa* has long ascidia, petioled at the base, reaching 12in (30cm) in height. Also notable are *H. heterodoxa* var. *exappendiculata*, which has pink flowers; *H. heterodoxa* var. *glabra*, which has white flowers and a complete absence of hairs on the inner wall of its ascidia at the top; and *H. heterodoxa* var. *heterodoxa*, which has flowers varying from white to pink and green pitchers, lightly tinted red. *H. minor* is a dwarf species, with pitchers measuring only 1½-3in (4-8cm) in height. *H. ionasi*, on the other hand, has large pitchers as high as 20in (50cm) set in a rosette; the flowers are white and become pink or red with age. The pubescent pitchers of

H. neblinae are about 10in (25cm); the flowers are white and turn pink. Finally, *H. tatei* has pitchers 14in (35cm) tall which grow in tufts, on top of each other; the flowers are white at first, becoming red.

Heliamphora minor in its natural habitat in Venezuela. The flower stalks, a beautiful red colour, stand well above the ascidia; × 0.2.

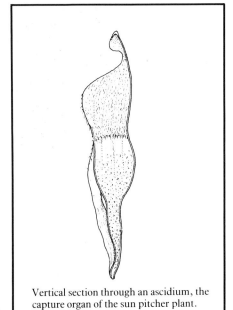

Vertical section through an ascidium, the capture organ of the sun pitcher plant. The beak-line operculum is a distinguishing feature.

Prey

Because of the shape of the traps, the prey is mainly winged insects such as flies, wasps and bees.

Passive pitfall trap

Sarracenia flava

Yellow trumpet

Family Sarraceniaceae.
Genus The genus *Sarracenia* comprises 8 species.
Common names Yellow trumpet; French, *Sarracène à fleurs jaunes*.
Origin Southwestern United States (from Virginia to Florida, especially on coastal plains).

	Size	1ft-3ft 3in (30cm-1m)
	Exposure	half shade or full sun
	Cultivation	in pots
	Humidity	high
	Temperature	up to 37°C
	Flowers	spring
	Life span	indefinite

History and etymology

Sarracenia flava was introduced into France in 1752 from the American continent. The species name, *flava*, means yellow in Latin. It refers not only to the colour of the flowers but also to the dominant tint of the whole of the plant.

Habitat

This species is found in damp places, often in the presence of sphagnum mosses. It can also be seen on open ground growing among other short plants, and, more rarely, in areas of light woodland.

Description

Dimensions The leaves, shaped like tubular trumpets, are erect and are 1ft-3ft 3in (30cm-1mm) in height.
Morphology The rhizome, which grows at the surface of the soil, produces several heads; the new leaves develop from these, while the oldest ones rot and die. The erect leaves are thick and firm, which makes them resistant to storms. They are veined and joined along their edges to form a longitudinal 'wing'. They are shaped like long narrow trum-

pets and are surmounted by a lid, a large appendage narrowing at the base, and oval or nearly round, which partially covers the entrance to the trumpet. At the of summer, rudimentary leaves, called phyllodes, form; they are flat and have a small limb. The leaves survive throughout the winter.
Character *S. flava* is a passive plant – its trap does not move. Insects are attracted by nectar produced by glands on the undersurface of the operculum,

Flower of *Sarracenia flava*. The pistil, shaped like an upside-down umbrella, is surrounded by pendant petals.

and by the brilliant colours of the leaves, Downward-pointing hairs are situated on the lid and inside the trumpet. Any escape for insects venturing inside is therefore impossible. Victims have no alternative but to make their way towards the bottom of the trap, where they end up being digested by enzymes and bacteria.

Flowers The flowers are borne on stalks high enough to stand clear of the foliage. They are large, regular, and of variable colour (bright yellow, yellow-green, or even cream).

Ornamental effect Besides its unusual foliage, the large leaves gives *S. flava* its decorative value.

Life span Its rhizomes allow the plant to reproduce continually, thus giving it an indefinite life span.

Reproduction

Sexual reproduction In the wild, insects pollinate *Sarracenia*. The flower is so structured that the insect must cross-fertilize the plants, it being unable to use that particular flower's pollen: the flower is in an inverted position and its ovary adjoins the stalk at the top. The ovary continues into a style, shaped like a five-pointed umbrella, each point having a single, tiny stigma. Above this, around the ovary, are the stamens, whose ripe pollen, at the slightest movement, falls into the umbrella but not on to the stigmas. The five petals, which are suspended around the style, leave any insect coming to gather nectar only the smallest hole, near the stigmas. The insect, usually a bee or some other

Hymenoptera, is attracted by the nectar glands situated at the base of the petals. It enters the flower by lifting a petal and brushes against one of the stigmas, depositing on it some of the pollen on its body from the previous flower. During its visit, it gathers pollen from the stamens or the umbrella. To escape from the flower, it lifts a petal, using the widest exit, between the points of the umbrella. In so doing, it does not deposit any pollen on that flower's stigmas, but carries it to the next flower. In order to imitate what happens in nature and to obtain fertile seeds when

Sarracenia flava plants in cultivation. The traps, or ascidia, are shaped like long, narrow trumpets. The flower stalks are generally rather higher; × 0.5.

cultivating, it is necessary to cross-fertilize. Take the pollen from the stamen of one flower using a brush or feather and deposit it on the stigmas of the flower to be fertilized. Keep the seeds in the refrigerator over the winter, at between 3° and 7°C. Sow them in seed trays filled with damp, sieved peat and

*S*arracenia flava
Yellow trumpet

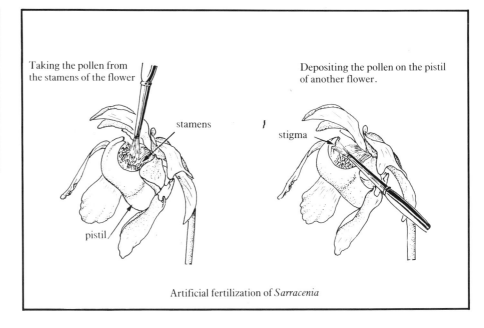

Taking the pollen from the stamens of the flower

Depositing the pollen on the pistil of another flower.

stamens

stigma

pistil

Artificial fertilization of *Sarracenia*

watered with a fungicide. Humidity must remain constant and the temperature must never drop below 18°C. Thin out the plants as they grow.

Asexual reproduction Reproduction by asexual means can be performed in different ways, in particular by simply dividing the plants (see also, 'Asexual reproduction' in other species of *Sarracenia*). When the plants have several heads, they can be separated by cutting the rhizomes into sections at least 1in (2.5cm) long, taking the roots along with each of the heads. Treat the cut parts with a fungicide before planting them. This operation can be performed only with fairly strong and mature plants and must be done in spring, at a temperature of at least 18°C.

Hybridization

Species of the genus *Sarracenia* are easily hybridized and many cross-fertilizations can take place, not only artifically but also in their original sites where several species co-habit. But these natural crossings, which can make identification difficult, are only rarely observed. For such a phenomenon to happen, flowers from different species have to open at the same time; it is also necessary for their colours, their dimensions, and their nectars to attract the same pollina-

ting insects. In cultivation, hybridization consists of pollinating the mother plant using pollen from the plant chosen for a partner. Use the same procedure as for a cross-fertilization between flowers of the same species (see 'Sexual reproduction'). Cover the fertilized flower with muslin to avoid any further pollina-

Different *Sarracenia flava* plants growing wild in Florida. The species is easily distinguished from the surrounding vegetation, thanks to its long ascidia surmounted with a hood; × 0.2.

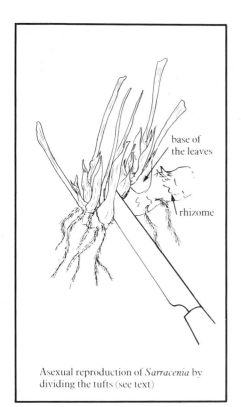

base of the leaves

rhizome

Asexual reproduction of *Sarracenia* by dividing the tufts (see text)

Prey

The majority of prey caught consists of flies of all types and sizes, as well as wasps, bees, and other related insects.

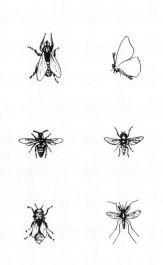

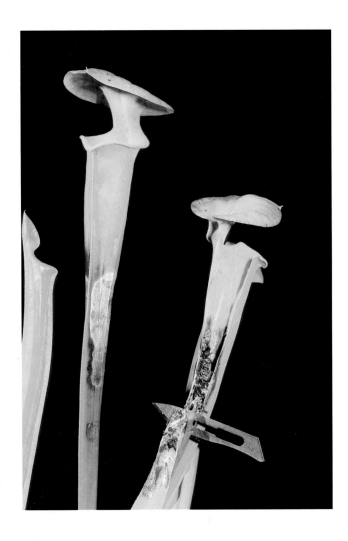

tion by insects. Finally label the plant, noting both parents (the seed-bearing or mother plant first) as well as the date the operation was performed. (See p.140 for the list of principal hybrids of the genus *Sarracenia*.)

Cultivation

Compost For compost use live or dead sphagnum moss, with perhaps some peat; river sand or perlite, to one fifth of the total volume, can also be added. Repotting must be done in spring. *Sarracenia* obtain their own fertilizers by catching insects and there is no need to use any supplementary fertilizers.

Watering The compost must be kept very damp throughout the whole growth period. The water must contain no chlorine or calcium.

Light *S. flava* can be grown in the open. Exposure to the sun gives the plant a bright colouring and prevents attack by fungi.

Temperature The species can withstand frost. Nevertheless, high temperatures do not do any harm as long as the compost remains very wet.

Rest If the plant is kept at a low temperature in winter, its foliage disappears. In a heated place, constant growth can be maintained throughout the year.

Pests and diseases

Aphids can sometimes settle on the traps or on the flowers. Fungi can also cover the surface of the traps. (For treatment see pp.28–9.)

Varieties

S. flava var. *atropurpurea*, also called *S. flava* var. *sanguinea*, is a semi-dwarf variety; the upper part of the ascidium and the operculum are strikingly veined with purple. *S. flava* var. *crispata* is

Drawing (left): the internal walls of *Sarracenia* have hairs that prevent prey from turning back; photo (above): vertical slice through an ascidium of *Sarracenia flava* revealing the remains of captured prey; × 0.7.

distinguishable by its green ascidia with a prominent wing and by its white-petalled flowers. *S. flava* var. *gigantea* reaches over 3ft (1m) in height and its ascidia are 4-6in (10-15cm) in diameter, while *S. flava* var. *minima* is a dwarf plant. Finally, there is *S. flava* var. *ornata*, with greenish yellow ascidia, veined and spotted with dark reddish-purple, which can reach 6in (15cm) in diameter.

Sarracenia leucophylla

Passive pitfall trap

White trumpet

Family Sarraceniaceae.
Genus The genus *Sarracenia* comprises 8 species.
Common names White trumpet or white-topped pitcher plant; French, *Sarracène blanc*.
Origin United States (southwest Georgia, northwest Florida, and to the west as far as Mississippi).

	Size	*8-37in (20-95cm)*
	Exposure	*half shade or full sun*
	Cultivation	*in pots*
	Humidity	*high*
	Temperature	*up to 37°C*
	Flowers	*spring*
	Life span	*indefinite*

History and etymology

Sarracenia leucophylla – the specific name means white leaves – was first recorded in 1829. It was discovered by the American botanist Chapman, near the town of Appalachicola in Florida.

Habitat

S. leucophylla is abundant in swampy meadows in its native habitat. It forms very spectacular groups of plants.

Description

Dimensions The leaves, folded into the shape of a trumpet, are 8-37in (20-95cm) in height. The flowers are 2-3in (5-8cm) in diameter.
Morphology The leaves are attached to a rhizome growing on the surface of the soil. They are folded around to form a kind of trumpet, narrow at the base and progressively wider towards the top. The wing, the joint line between the two edges, is narrow. The pitchers are green at the base and crowned with white with green or red veins on the upper part. Phyllodes, or pitchers reduced to the state of simple leaves, form at the end of summer and, if the winter is very cold, the foliage disappears completely.

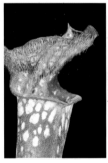 

Upper part of the trap of a *Sarracenia leucophylla*; the operculum is covered with hairs; × 1.2.

Vertical section of the ascidium, lined with very fine hairs and full of prey; × 1.2.

Character The pitcher is surmounted by a lid, an extension of the leaf blades. This, when erect, is spherical in shape with wavy edges. The undersurface of the lid has nectar glands to attract insects. When these land, they are directed towards the entrance of the pitcher by numerous, downward-pointing, fine, silky hairs. They die of exhaustion and are then digested by the bacteria and enzymes secreted at the base of the ascidium.
Flowers One flower opens in spring at the end of the flower stalk. The flowers are purple and they give off a pleasant scent.

Ornamental effect Its large white pitchers, veined green or red, make *S. leucophylla* a very beautiful species.
Life span The presence of a rhizome, which survives even a cold winter, means that the plant is perennial.

Reproduction

Sexual reproduction The structure of the flower, and especially the umbrella shape of the pistil, prevents any chance of self-fertilization in natural conditions (see *Sarracenia flava*: 'Sexual reproduction'). When cultivating, this constraint must always be borne in mind and an artificial cross-fertilization performed: take the pollen from the stamens of one flower using a brush or feather. The fertilized flower rapidly loses its petals and sepals and the flower stalk stands up so as to carry the fruit vertically. Collect the seeds in autumn and put them in the refrigerator at between 3° and 7°C. They should be sown in spring on damp peat and watered with a fungicide. It is not necessary to cover the seeds but it is important that the ambient temperature be above 18°C.
Asexual reproduction There are several methods of reproducing this species by asexual means (see under other species of *Sarracenia*). One technique

consists of clearing the rhizomes of all its leaves and, with a sharp blade, making cuts in it deep enough to reach the centre, about every 1¼in (3cm). Then treat it with a fungicide and place it on the surface of the compost. Roots will form and shoots will develop in place of each of the leaves that grew from the rhizome. The temperature must stay above 18°C.

Hybridization

See p.140 for the list of the main hybrids of *Sarracenia*.

Cultivation

Compost Use a sphagnum-based compost. Peat may be added and up to one fifth river sand or perlite. It is not necessary to use fertilizers. Repot when growth returns.

Watering The compost must be kept very damp during the growth period. Watering should be reduced in winter but kept constant. The water must be as pure as possible, rainwater being the most appropriate.

Light The plants withstand exposure to direct sunlight, which gives them vivid colours.

Temperature. *S. leucophylla* is a tender plant; it should be left out only in the mildest of winters. If temperatures are high, it is very important to keep the compost wet.

Rest Even with this species, from a relatively hot climate, foliage usually disappears in winter, except when cultivated in a greenhouse.

Pests and diseases

Fungi sometimes cause the ascidia to turn brown. Aphids may also settle on the plants. (For treatment, see pp.28–9.)

Varieties

S. leucophylla var. *alba* has large ascidia, white over roughly half of the upper part, and with reddish-purple veins. *S. leucophylla* var. *rubra* is not as large and the upper part of its ascidia is purple and white. *S. leucophylla* var. *undulata* is distinguished by its operculum, whose edges are very undulating.

Sarracenia leucophylla in the wild in its native Florida; × 0.2.

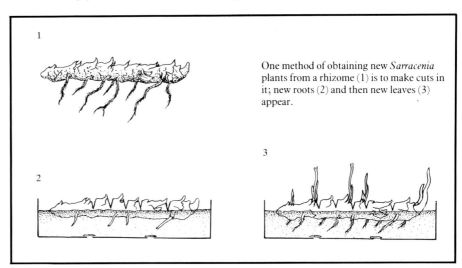

One method of obtaining new *Sarracenia* plants from a rhizome (1) is to make cuts in it; new roots (2) and then new leaves (3) appear.

Prey

S. leucophylla attracts and catches large numbers of insects – mostly winged insects such as flies, wasps and bees.

Passive pitfall trap

Sarracenia minor

Hooded pitcher plant

Family Sarraceniaceae.
Genus The genus *Sarracenia* comprises 8 species.
Common names Hooded pitcher plant; French, *Sarracène minor*.
Origin United States (from southern North Carolina to northern Florida).

Size		4-32in (10-80cm)
Exposure		half shade or full sun
Cultivation		in pots
Humidity		high
Temperature		up to 37°C
Flowers		spring
Life span		indefinite

History and etymology

The earliest record of *Sarracenia minor*, in the form of an engraving, dates back to 1576, but the plant was first described only in 1788. It was thought then that the plant came from dry regions, where it struggled to develop. Since the first examples of the species were only small, this would explain its name. However, in damp areas, the leaves can reach 28in (70cm). The same species has also been called *variolaris* because of the whitish blotches, resembling smallpox rash, on the upper part of the traps. Finally, one botanist gave the species the name *aduncus*, meaning hooked, because of the shape of the very top of the traps.

Habitat

S. minor grows in savanna and in relatively sparse pine forests. Although it is generally found in regions drier than those inhabited by other *Sarracenia*, it also enjoys damp sites – it is noticeable in fact, that the best-developed plants are those growing in damp situations, in sphagnum mosses.

Description

Dimensions The leaves, modified into traps, are 4-32in (10-80cm) long.
Morphology The leaves, which grow directly from the rhizome, are folded longitudinally to form the trumpets – narrow, almost perfectly cylindrical tubes constricting into petioles at the base. The joint, or wing, between the two edges of the folded leaf, is membranous. It is green, becoming red or yellow in the sun and reddish-brown when the plant ages. Some spots, transparent due to an absence of chlorophyll, appear on the upper part of the trumpet and allow light to pass.
Character The trap is surmounted by a lid shaped like a hood, with delicate red veins. It is sessile and curves right over the entrance to the trap, partially covering it. Its inner surface is supplied with nectar glands, which attract and intoxicate insects. Those that risk entering the trap are unable to turn back because of downward-pointing hairs. They become exhausted and end up being assimilated by the digestive glands, containing bacteria, at the bottom of the trap.
Flowers The solitary flowers are borne on stalks that are shorter then the foliage; they are quite tall and yellow. Their narrow petals spread outwards, instead of hanging as in other species. They have no scent.

Ornamental effect Small windows at the top of the traps, containing no chlorophyll, allow light to pass inside and make them quite distinctive.
Life span Thanks to the rhizome, from which the leaves develop and which stays alive even when the foliage dies, the plant's life span is indefinite.

Reproduction

Sexual reproduction If the flowers have not been fertilized by insects, as when cultivating indoors, an artificial cross-fertilization has to be made to obtain fertile seeds. This means taking the pollen from the numerous stamens of one flower and transporting it with a small brush or feather to the stigmas of another flower (see *Sarracenia flava*: 'Sexual reproduction'). Seeds take at least three months to ripen and are collected in autumn. Then they must be placed in the cold over winter; a refrigerator kept at 3° to 7°C is quite suitable. The seeds, set out in spring on the surface of damp peat, must be treated with a fungicide. The temperature must then stay above 18°C. It takes about five years to develop an adult plant.
Asexual reproduction As with the other species of the genus, *S. minor* can be reproduced asexually by various methods (for this, see also the other

species of *Sarracenia*). One method is to produce new shoots on the rhizome by cutting off the leading shoot along with 1in (2.5cm) of the rhizome. (The leading shoot is at the end of the rhizome.)

Take off any remaining ascidia from the rhizome; secondary shoots will grow to replace them and these will form new plants. The end-piece can be used as a cutting (see *Sarracenia purpurea*: 'Sexual reproduction'). If the rhizome is too short to take off the leading shoot, simply cut off the bud. This technique can be used only with plants that are sufficiently developed and a temperature of at least 18°C is needed.

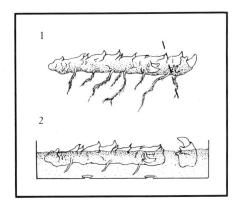

Asexual reproduction of *Sarracenia* by suppressing the leading shoot (see text).

Hybridization

See p.140 for the list of the main hybrids of *Sarracenia*, especially *S. minor*.

Cultivation

Compost *S. minor* should preferably be cultivated in a sphagnum-based compost, but peat, with one fifth river sand or perlite, is satisfactory. No fertilizers are necessary. The plants must be repotted in spring in a container big enough for the rhizome to continue its development throughout the year. *S. minor* is the only *Sarracenia* species whose rhizome does not partly emerge from the surface of the compost.

Watering The compost must be kept quite wet during the growth period and drier but still damp during the winter rest. If possible, use rainwater with an acidity of betweeen 5 and 6 pH.

Light Like other *Sarracenia*, this species withstands direct sunlight when cultivated outdoors. However, light shade is required when under glass.

A *Sarrracenia minor* plant in flower in the spring. The traps vary greatly in size; × 0.6.

Temperature It is advisable not to subject *S. minor* to frost, even though the species is resistant to light frosts. High temperatures can be tolerated as long as the compost stays wet.

Rest The foliage may or may not disappear according to whether or not the plants have been kept in a heated greenhouse.

Pests and diseases

Pests common to all species of *Sarracenia* can attack this species, particularly fungi, which form on the ascidia. Aphids are more rare. Finally, certain caterpillars can perforate the traps and even, in the American species, be found inside the rhizomes. (For treatment, see pp.28–31.)

Mature fruit of *Sarracenia minor*, in autumn: the seeds can be gathered but they must undergo a period of cold before being sown; × 7.

Prey

S. minor grows in areas that are less damp than those that are home to other species of its genus. Besides winged insects, which all *Sarracenia* catch, *S. minor* also traps large numbers of ants.

Sarracenia psittacina

Passive pitfall trap

Parrot pitcher plant

Family Sarraceniaceae.
Genus The genus *Sarracenia* comprises 8 species.
Common names Parrot pitcher plant; French, *Sarracène à bec de perroquet*.
Origin United States (southern Georgia, northern Florida, southern Lousiana, and Mississippi).

Size		*2-12in (5-30cm)*
Exposure		*half shade or full sun*
Cultivation		*in pots*
Humidity		*high*
Temperature		*up to 37°C*
Flowers		*spring*
Life span		*indefinite*

History and etymology

The species was introduced into Europe in 1860 and mentioned in the *Gardener's Chronicle* in 1866. The specific name derives from the Greek *psittakos*, 'parrot', because the very top of the ascidium is shaped like a parrot's beak.

Habitat

The parrot pitcher plant grows in wet or even swampy areas and in particular in biologically poor marshes in pine forests. Other plants often grow alongside it, particularly when the site is wet and often submerged during the rains.

Description

Dimensions The leaves, modified into a trap, can measure 2-12in (5-30cm) in length.
Morphology The pitchers, which are leaves folded round in the shape of a trumpet, are decumbent; they grow from the rhizome and are set in a rosette. It is this feature that distinguishes *Sarracenia psittacina* from all other species of the same genus. Along their front they have a longitudinal wing, which is in fact the joint between the two edges of the folded leaf. This structure is wider at the top. The upper part of the pitcher extends into a curved appendage, looking rather like a parrot's head, whose summit ends in a point. It is green at the base, has red veins in the middle section, and is completely red on the upper part, which is exposed to the sun. As with *S. minor*, white patches having no chlorophyll are present in this region. The pitchers are hardy; they do not die during winter.
Character The pitcher's entrance hole is round and about ³⁄₁₆in (5mm) in diameter. It is surrounded by a sort of rolled rim, which, together with tangled downward-pointing hairs inside the pitcher, mean no retreat for any little animal venturing into the trap. Since the plant lives in places that are often underwater, it is usually aquatic animals that are captured.
Flowers The relatively small flowers are deep red and have a pleasant scent. They open in spring.
Ornamental effect The decorative value of *S. pssittacina* comes particularly from its rather special shape and the rich colouring of its traps.
Life span In good conditions, life expectancy is unlimited, as with the other *Sarracenia*.

Reproduction

Sexual reproduction The flower structure of *S. psittacina* is such that, in natural conditions, pollinating insects cannot fertilize a flower with its own pollen (see *Sarracenia flava*: 'Sexual reproduction'.) In cultivation, obtaining fertile seeds necessitates cross-fertilization, which consists of taking the pollen from one flower and placing it on the stigmas of another. This can be done using a feather or a brush. A short time after fertilization the flower loses its sepals and petals. When the fruit turns brown in autumn the seeds are collected. They are put to dry and then kept in the cold – between 3° and 7°C, in a refrigerator – over winter. They are sown in spring on damp peat and the seed beds then treated with a fungicide.

The compost must remain permanently damp and a temperature of at least 18°C should be maintained. Prick out when the seedlings have sprouted two cotyledons into seed trays of the same compost as used for sowing. When the plants are bigger, plant them out in small pots or jars. The time needed to obtain an adult plant is about five years.
Asexual reproduction One of the asexual reproduction techniques applicable to *S. psittacina* consists of taking cuttings of the traps (for this, see also the other species of *Sarracenia*). Carefully

take off the ascidia to be used, along with a small part of the rhizome and some roots. Put them in a damp sphagnum moss and treat them with a fungicide. Growth hormones may help root development.

Hybridization

See p.140 for the list of principal hybrids of the genus *Sarracenia*.

Cultivation

Compost Use sphagnum moss, perhaps mixed with peat and, in amounts not exceeding one fifth of the total, river sand or perlite. Plants must be repotted in spring; they may suffer or even die if repotted out of season.
Watering The compost must be kept constantly wet during the growth periods; in winter the plant must be

Sarracenia psittacina in cultivation. The traps, with their very small openings, have a very characteristic shape; × 0.3.

kept completely immersed in water, which must be free of chlorine and calcium and have a pH of 5 or 6.
Light In outdoor cultivation, the plants can be exposed to direct sunlight. Their colours will be all the more brilliant. They will need slight shade if cultivated in a greenhouse.
Temperature Protect *S. psittacina* from frost. High temperatures, up to a ceiling of about 37°C, are bearable as long as the compost is kept wet.
Rest The leaves remain through the winter.

Pests and diseases

Pests of the parrot pitcher plant can be aphids but, above all, *Oïdium or Botrytis* fungi attack *S. psittacina*. (For treatment see pp.28–9).

Asexual reproduction of **Sarracenia** *using the traps as cuttings*

To use *Sarracenia* traps for cuttings, pull them off very carefully, along with a small piece of the rhizome and some of the attached roots.

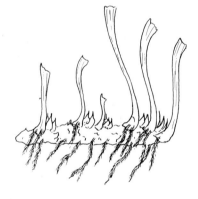

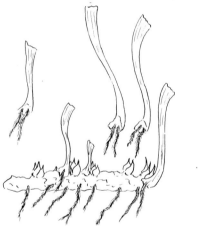

Prey

In natural conditions, the traps are often partly submerged in water and they catch small aquatic invertebrates. Prey can also be winged insects.

Sarracenia purpurea

Purple pitcher plant

Family Sarraceniaceae.
Genus The genus *Sarracenia* comprises 8 species.
Common names Purple pitcher plant or northern pitcher plant; French, *Sarracène pourpre*.
Origin North America (in large areas over the northern parts of the continent, along the Atlantic coast as far south as Florida, and from Georgia to Mississippi).

Size		4-8in (10-20cm)
Exposure		half shade or full sun
Cultivation		in pots
Humidity		high
Temperature		up to 37°C
Flowers		spring and the beginning of summer
Life span		indefinite

History and etymology

Sarracenia purpurea was the first *Sarracenia* species to be introduced into Europe; it was imported to England in 1640. A plate of it can be seen in Diderot's *Encyclopédie*.

The name *purpurea* was attributed to it because of the purplish tint of its flowers, but purple is also the dominant colour of the whole of the plant when exposed to sun.

Habitat

In the wild, the purple pitcher grows in marshy areas.

Description

Dimensions The leaves, forming the traps, are 4-8in (10-20cm) long and the flower stalk is 12-16in (30-40cm) in height; it is surmounted by a flower up to 4in (10cm) in diameter.

Morphology Each plant is made up of numerous sessile leaves, which come directly from the rhizome. These leaves are short and folded in such a way that they form a tube, narrowing at the base, wider and bulbous around the middle, and rather constricted at the top, around the opening. The wing, which is the seam between the two edges of the joined leaves, is slightly bowed. The whole organ is green in colour on its frontal part, possibly veined with purple or even completely purple depending on the amount of exposure to the sun. As with other species of *Sarracenia*, the internal structure of the traps can be divided into four distinct zones. The upper part is supplied with nectar glands, which attract insects and are set between the downward-pointing hairs, making escape for prey impossible. The second zone, situated below the first, is smooth; it also has nectar glands, as has the third zone, which is smooth and glabrous. The lower zone has downward-pointing hairs that retain the prey; here, digestive enzymes are secreted and bacteria are also present. Captured insects cannot be completely digested and their non-assimilated parts gather at the base of the trap as a blackish mass.

Character The traps are passive. Made up of leaves folded round on themselves, they are topped by a sessile, heart-shaped lid, which points upwards. The lid surrounds about two thirds of the entrance of the trap. The remaining one third of the periphery is thicker and often light brown in colour. The surface of the lid is smooth on the outside and covered with fine, whitish hairs on the inside. These point downwards towards the inside of the trap, where there are

Vertical section through the trap of a *S. purpurea*; at the bottom, the zone having digestive glands; × 1.3.

Sarracenia purpurea var. *venosa*, one of the natural variations of *S. purpurea* to be found in the wild; × 0.8.

more. Insects attracted by the nectar glands land on this area and are forced to head for the base of the trumpet. There they die and their dissolvable parts are gradually digested.

Flowers Situated on the end of its stalk, the flower is regular. As with all *Sarracenia*, the corolla is made up of five oval, very large petals, sunk inwards at the ends. There are numerous stamens, each composed of a short filament terminating in a simple rounded anther. The ovary is almost spherical and is surmounted by a short cylindrical style, itself topped by a shield in the shape of a five-cornered umbrella covering the stamens. Underneath the ends of each of these corners is a stigma. The fruit is a capsule of five compartments holding the tiny seeds. *S. purpurea* has a large flower; it is usually a rather dark purple, occasionally pink. It emits a strong scent, which changes through the day.

Ornamental effect Plants grown in the sun turn a beautiful purple.

Life span This is indefinite in good conditions of cultivation; the rhizomes ensure the continuation of the species when the foliage disappears.

A *Sarracenia purpurea* flower. As in all species of *Sarracenia*, the flower stalk curves down. The large petals, shaped like an inside-out umbrella, shroud the pistil. Flower colour varies even within the same species, but is usually reddish-purple; × 1.

Reproduction

Sexual reproduction Insects are the natural means of transporting the pollen from one flower to another, thus ensuring cross-fertilization. To imitate this and perform an artificial fertilization, pollen must be taken from one flower with a small brush and deposited on the stigmas of another. This latter rapidly withers and its ovary gradually enlarges. Collect the seeds in autumn, dry them, and keep them in a temperature of 3° to 7°C over the winter. Sow them, in spring, on wet peat. Water with a fungicide solution. From then on, keep the temperature above 18°C.

Asexual reproduction *S. purpurea* can be reproduced by taking rhizome cuttings (see also the other species of *Sarracenia* for this). This method means cutting the rhizome into sections at least 1in (2.5cm) long, taking care not to damage the roots. Then treat the cut parts with a fungicide and place them horizontally on the surface of the compost, spreading out the roots. Finally, cover them with a layer of sphagnum moss or peat to ½in (1cm) and keep it all at a minimum temperature of 18° to 20°C.

Sarracenia purpurea

Purple pitcher plant

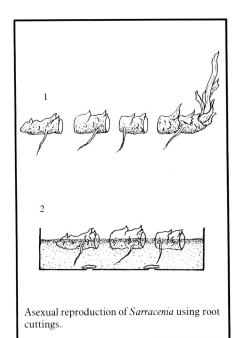

Asexual reproduction of *Sarracenia* using root cuttings.

Hybridization

See p.140 for the list of the principal species of *Sarracenia*.

Cultivation

Compost For the compost, use sphagnum, perhaps mixed with peat. Unlike other species of the same genus, *Sarracenia purpurea* is happy in a soil which is not too acid. It is pointless to use fertilizers.

Taking cuttings from the rhizome involves cutting it into 1-1¼ in (2.5-3 cm) sections (1). These are then treated (2).

Watering The pots can be kept in a bed of water for the whole of the growing period. Reduce the amount of water but never allow the compost to dry out. Use rainwater if possible.

Light Outdoors, the plants can withstand exposure to direct sunlight, but greenhouse cultivations must be slightly shaded.

Temperature. Like *S. flava*, *S. purpurea* tolerates frost. When the temperature is high, in summer, make sure the compost remains very wet.

Rest In winter, under natural conditions, when the temperature drops very low, the plant loses its leaves. The foliage returns in spring from the rhizome.

Pests and diseases

Be wary of aphids and especially fungi (for treatment, see pp.28–9). In America, certain populations of *Sarracenia* are attacked by the caterpillars of three species of a butterfly of the *Exyra* genus.

Sarracenia purpurea can tolerate frost. Here, the ascidia are still visible under a thin layer of snow; × 0.5.

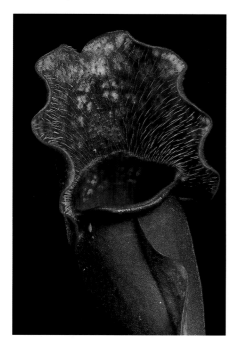

Entrance of the trap of *S. purpurea* var. *purpurea*; × 1.5.

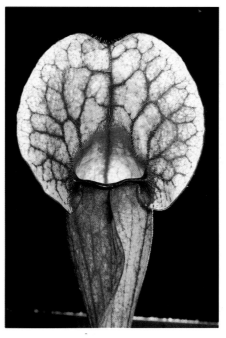

Entrance of the trap of *S. purpurea* var. *venosa*; × 1.5.

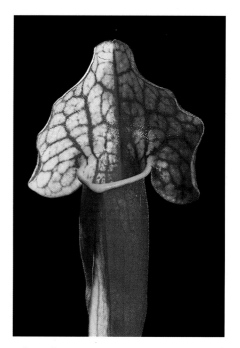

S. catesbaei, natural hybrid of *S. purpurea*; × 1.1.

The butterfly is able to hide in the traps without being caught. In each trap, the female lays an egg which quickly changes into a devastating larva. It signals its presence by weaving a web across the entrance of the trap, preventing not only insects but also rainwater from getting inside. The caterpillar feeds on the internal walls of the trap, which loses its effectiveness. The larva pierces two holes above the level of its droppings, which accumulate at the bottom; the lower of the two holes serves to let out the water while the upper one allows it to escape when it has transformed into the adult insect. Larvae of this type withstand frost and go from one trap to another. They are themselves prey to certain birds which are able to locate them, but only in small numbers. However, they are also killed off by fires which otherwise do not harm the plant since it is able to regenerate itself via the rhizome.

Varieties

There are several varieties of the species, depending on their respective habitats. *S. purpurea* var. *purpurea* is a northern variety, found between New Jersey and Labrador. The leaves are folded into long, narrow trumpets; they are green in summer and turn brown in winter. The flowers have various tints – bronze, pink, or yellowish-green. In natural conditions, this variety forms tufts, sometimes exceeding 3ft (1m) in diameter. It is found in the form of floating masses on the edges of lakes or swamps. It has adapted to grow in either acid or alkaline waters. It is seen especially around the Great Lakes. *S. purpurea* var. *venosa* is the southern variety. It is a native of New Jersey, but also grows in the whole of the region extending south as far down as Louisana. The leaves are folded into shorter but fatter trumpets than those of the *purpurea* variety, from which it can also be distinguished by its pubescence.

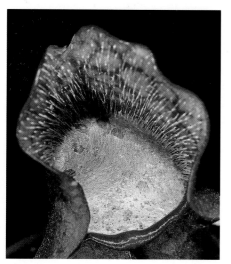

Web woven by the caterpillar of a butterfly (genus *Exyra*) at the entrance to an ascidium of *S. purpurea*; × 2.

Prey

Prey is flying insects, mostly flies, bees and wasps.

Cephalotus follicularis

Albany pitcher plant

Family Cephalotaceae; this family comprises only the *Cephalotus* genus.

Genus The genus *Cephalotus* contains only one species, *C. follicularis*.

Common names Albany pitcher plant; French, *Plante carnivore d'Albany* or *plante carnivore australienne*.

Origin The town of Albany, in the extreme southwest of Australia.

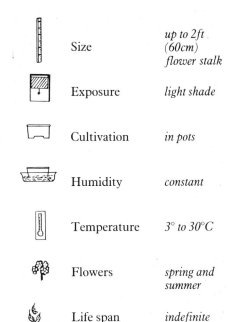

Size	up to 2ft (60cm) flower stalk
Exposure	light shade
Cultivation	in pots
Humidity	constant
Temperature	3° to 30°C
Flowers	spring and summer
Life span	indefinite

History and etymology

The species was discovered during an expedition to southwest Australia 'in search of the Peruvian woman', led by the navigator Entrecasteaux in 1792. La Billardière, the expedition's botanist, described the plant in 1806. It was introduced into Europe – into England's Kew Gardens – in 1823. The generic name derives from the Greek *kephalotus*, meaning having a head, which refers to the anthers; the species name, *follicularis*, which means small bag, refers to the shape of the ascidia.

Habitat

A native of damp or marshy peatland that is often submerged in water, in the wild *Cephalotus follicularis* lives surrounded by grasses. Plants exposed to sun are not as strong as those growing in shade. Nevertheless, the mahogany colouring can be obtained only with some exposure to sun, so the ideal is to cultivate the plant in a lightly shaded area until it is fully developed and then to expose it gradually to the sun. The winter foliage can disappear completely and slight frosts in no way affect its ability to regrow its foliage. Spring growth does not usually involve the development of traps; these form in summer, when insects are more plentiful.

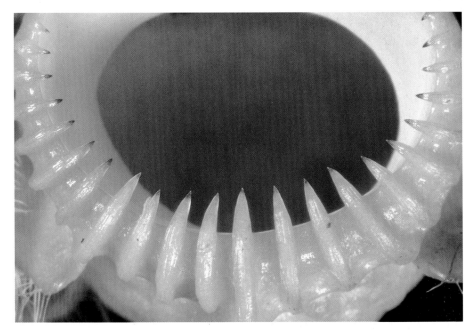

Sharp teeth around the entrance to the trap of *Cephalotus follicularis*, preventing prey from turning back; × 8.

Description

Dimensions The longest leaves can reach 5in (12cm). The largest urns can be 2in (5cm) high – 3in (8cm) in exceptional cases – by ¾-1¼in (2-3cm) in diameter. The flower stalks can bear a hundred or so very small flowers reaching about 2ft (60cm) in height.

Morphology *C. follicularis* is a plant with a very strong, central, ramified root, from which the rosette of leaves grows. These may be with or without urns, according to the state of growth and the season. Only the leaves with urns are insectivorous. The un-urned leaves, which have a normal limb, a lengthened oblong, develop in spring; those with urns appear next, during the more favourable time of the year, when

When *Cephalotus follicularis* is cultivated in filtered sunlight its urns are coloured a deeper red; × 2.

the plant can catch the maximum number of insects.

The urns are surmounted by a lid and bear some resemblance to the *Nepenthes* urns. The petiole is set at right angles to the vertical axis of the urn; the opening or mouth of the urn is edged around its periphery by a shiny rim, or peristome, with longitudinal ridges, half-ring shaped; each half-ring stands proud of the peristome and ends in a sharp point on the inner margin of the opening. These ribs number about twenty-three or twenty-four to each urn. The rings and their teeth are larger at the front than near the lid. The pocket of the urn has three exterior, longitudinal prominences. The central one, in front of the urn, is the most important; in cross-section it is T-shaped. Both the others also have this shape, but not as pronounced. All three have long cilia along their edges. The lid partly covers the trap opening, at an angle of roughly 25°.

Character *C. follicularis* is a passive plant and the lid cannot move at all. It is rather like a convex dome, coloured with alternating brown-red and pale green stripes; there are windows in this zone, because of the absence of chlorophyll in some parts. Insects are attracted to it, as with *Darlingtonia* or certain *Sarracenia*. Numerous hairs cover the top surface and edge of the lid. Its inner wall is lined with nectar glands. The upper part of the trap on the inside is white, smooth, and slippery and it has digestive glands; the bottom has none.

Attracted by the nectar glands, insects enter over a very smooth peristome, lose their balance, and slip inside; they stand no chance of climbing up the inner wall once they have touched the liquid at the bottom of the trap, and, even if they manage on rare occasions to clamber back up to the peristome, they meet its insurmountable rim: it is death by drowning and their bodies are assimilated by enzymes secreted by the digestive glands and by bacteria present in the solution. Winged insects are lured by the operculum's windows, through which they think they can leave but they exhaust themselves vainly trying to escape.

Flowers The flower stalks carry numerous small flowers on panicles; they are regular and have a single perianth; the flowers are formed of six 1¼in (3mm) whitish-green sepals, twelve stamens, six of which are smaller than the others, and six free carpels, each one comprising a unilocular ovary (having one cavity) with a single ovule. The fruit is made up of six follicles and the seed contains albumen. The flowers appear in spring.

Ornamental effect *C. follicularis* is a

115

Cephalotus follicularis
Albany pitcher plant

plant curiosity because of the appearance of its urns, lined with many hairs, because of the purple colour of its opercula and their white or translucent windows.

Life span It is a hardy plant, either perennial or of continuous growth, depending on the conditions in which it is cultivated.

Reproduction

Sexual reproduction The flowers open each day in groups of three or four, for one month. Fertilize them, by transferring pollen from one flower to another, as they are flowering. The seeds take seven weeks to reach maturity and then they must undergo a cold spell of at least two months before they will germinate. A refrigerator temperature of 4° to 9°C is suitable. Then sow them on damp peat and spray with a fungicide. Germination may occur after only eight weeks, but it sometimes requires up to a year.

Asexual reproduction Leaf cuttings: use old leaves, with or without urns. Take them off carefully, retaining the whole of the petiole and cover the severed parts with a fungicide powder. Place them in peat or sphagnum, pushing half the petiole into the compost, or simply lay them on the compost, provided that it is sufficiently wet. Rhizome cuttings: divide the rhizomes into 1in (2-3 mm) sections and treat with a fungicide by soaking or powdering the cut parts. Place them horizontally in the peat or sphagnum and cover them to a depth of ⅜in (1cm). Keep the cultivation wet and the temperature at 21°C minimum for both types of cuttings. The young plants appear after one month. Separate them when their roots are well enough developed.

Hybridization

No hybridization has yet been recorded.

Cultivation

Compost The base compost is a mixture of half sphagnum and half peat, to which some river sand can be added. If used separately, live sphagnum seems preferable since the quality of peat varies. However, both types of compost give satisfactory results. Sphagnum moss must be cut when it becomes overgrown. Choose pots of a diameter large enough for good rhizome development.

Watering Keep the compost damp throughout the growing period, watering less in winter when the temperature drops. Preferably, rainwater should be used. Relative humidity must be between 60 and 80 per cent.

Light Keep the plants in light shade while they are developing, then expose them to the sun to give them a mahogany colour.

Temperature This can be anything between 3° and 30°C. This species does not mind high temperatures and, if kept at between 20° and 30°C, will remain in leaf. Below 7°C, parts above ground will disappear. The species can withstand light frosts and its rhizomes push up new shoots in spring.

Rest It is normal to observe a rest period even though continuous growth may be possible if the temperature remains above 20°C.

Pests and diseases

Cephalotus frequently die when attacked by *Botrytis*. A fungicide treatment will be needed in such cases. Aphids can also develop on the plants, but they are easy to spot and treat.

Urns of *Cephalotus follicularis* of different ages. On the urn to the left, the ribs, covered in hair, can be seen; × 2.5.

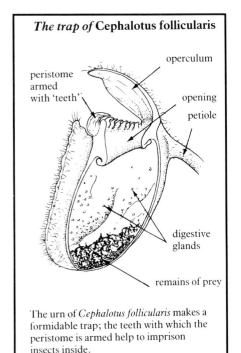

The trap of **Cephalotus follicularis**

peristome armed with 'teeth'

operculum

opening

petiole

digestive glands

remains of prey

The urn of *Cephalotus follicularis* makes a formidable trap; the teeth with which the peristome is armed help to imprison insects inside.

Flowers of *Cephalotus follicularis* are grouped in panicles. Each flower bears six almost colourless petals; × 12.

Below: unwary aphids venturing round the trap entrance of a *Cephalotus follicularis*. The ribs on the peristome are clearly visible, as well as the urn's longitudinal prominence; × 3.

Prey

All kinds of insects are caught. Ants in particular find their way into urns that lie partly on the soil and constitute a large proportion of the prey.

Passive pitfall trap

Nepenthes alata

Winged Nepenthes

Family Nepenthaceae.
Genus The genus *Nepenthes* comprises 72 species living in the wild.
Common name Winged Nepenthes.
Origin Borneo, Malaysia, Philippines, Sumatra.

Size	up to 13ft (4m)
Exposure	half shade
Cultivation	in pots or hanging baskets
Humidity	high
Temperature	10° to 25°C
Flowers	mostly in summer
Life span	indefinite

Etymology

The name of the species, *alata*, derives from the Latin *ala*, meaning wing – the traps or urns have two longitudinal, prominent wings, which are in fact expanded membranes.

Habitat

Being either terrestrial or epiphytic, the winged Nepenthes grows among grasses or shrubs, in sunny or shaded sites. The species is found at altitudes of between 1000 and 8000ft (300 and 2400m).

Description

Dimensions The branches, ⅛-⁵⁄₁₆in (4-8mm) in diameter, can climb up to 13ft (4m). The leaves at the base of the plant grow to 5in (13cm) in length by 1⅜in (3.5cm), while those on the climbing branches grow to a length of 10in (25cm). The inflorescence forms a bunch 4-16in (10-40cm) long.
Morphology The branches can be short, prostrate, or climbing; they are cylindrical or triangular in section. New shoots grow from the base of older plants and form rosettes of leaves. In general, the leaves differ according to their position on the plant. It is the same

with the urns that form the traps. There are three distinct categories of both leaf and urn – those at the base, those in the middle, and those on the climbing branches. The limb of the basal leaves is obtuse in shape, or even pointed. Unlike those situated higher up, these leaves are irregularly set on the branch. The intermediate leaves are fine, tough, and lance-shaped (resembling either a long, thin blade or a spoon-shaped one). The leaves on the climbing branches are similar; their petiole bears two narrow wings, which surround the branch. All leaves terminate in a tendril – a cylindrical-sectioned continuation of the central vein – which carries the trap. Like the leaves, the tendrils have different shapes.
Character The urns are passive traps in which the prey – mostly insects – drown after being attracted by the numerous nectar glands situated around the lid that leans over the urn. The victims are digested by bacteria present in the liquid at the bottom and assimiliated by the many digestive glands situated at this level. Morphologically, the urns differ from each other, particularly in the shape of their lids, but also in the length of the spur; this is a thick spine or thorn situated at the back of the hinge that joins the lid to the rest of the trap. On the intermediate urns the spine is ¹⁄₁₆-³⁄₁₆in (2-5mm) long; on the upper ones,

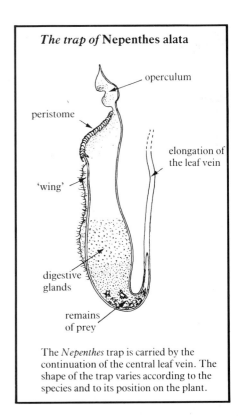

The trap of **Nepenthes alata**

operculum

peristome

elongation of the leaf vein

'wing'

digestive glands

remains of prey

The *Nepenthes* trap is carried by the continuation of the central leaf vein. The shape of the trap varies according to the species and to its position on the plant.

118

A *Nepenthes alata* out of its pot. This species produces urns readily; × 0.3.

Nepenthes alata
Winged Nepenthes

up to ⁵⁄₁₆in (8mm). The lower and intermediate urns, in addition, carry over their whole length two fringed wings, or expanded membranes; on the upper traps, these are replaced by genuine, prominent ribs. All the urns are pale green with brown-red patches.

Flowers The male inflorescence is in the form of an elongated bunch, 4-16in (10-40cm) long. The flowers are borne on ⁹⁄₁₆in (15mm) stalks; their sepals are oval. The female inflorescence is similar.

Ornamental effect It is the urns, with their two fringed wings, sometimes tinted red or purple, that give *Nepenthes alata* its ornamental value.

Life span Indefinite in good conditions of cultivation.

Reproduction

Sexual reproduction All *Nepenthes*, and *N. alata* in particular, are dioecious plants – in other words, the male and female flowers are on different plants. Obtaining seeds in cultivation means depositing the pollen from a male flower on to the stigma of a female flower using a brush or feather, or by bringing the anthers (at the ends of the stamens) of a male flower into contact with the stigma of a female flower. It is therefore necessary to have available both male and female flowers but, failing this, it is possible to save pollen in a plastic container in the refrigerator at between 3° and 6°C. The seeds reach maturity in four to five months. The capsules are loculicidal, meaning that the carpels split open longitudinally along the medial vein. There are large numbers of seeds (100 to 600 for the whole inflorescence). Like the pollen, they can be kept for three to six months if they are placed in a refrigerator, but it is best to sow them as soon as possible. Sow them in seed trays on the surface of fine peat and

treat them with fungicide. Keep the culture damp, and roughly between 10° and 25°C (18° to 30°C for low-altitude species). Germination takes place after one to three months. When the seedlings have two or three leaves, replant them in peat, spreading them out to provide room for further growth. In addition, they can be sown in vitro using the same procedures as those for orchid seeds.

Asexual reproduction The most common method for asexual reproduction is to take cuttings, if possible just before

growth is ready to return (see *Nepenthes maxima*: 'Asexual reproduction').

Hybridization

Nepenthes fertilize themselves easily and many hybrids were recorded during the last century. When different species occur on the same site they produce natural hybrids. Thus, *N. alata* is a parent of *Nepenthes × merrilliata* (*N. alata × N. merrilliana*) and of *Nepenthes × ventrata* (*N. alata × N. ventricosa*).

Nepenthes alata in its natural habitat, on the outskirts of Baguio, in the Philippines; × 0.2.

But other, cultivated, hybrids exist (see p.142 for the list of *Nepenthes* hybrids).

Cultivation

Compost A variety of composts can be used and they all give excellent results (see p.23). Periodically, the plants need to be repotted; take care not to damage the roots during this operation (see p. 25).

Watering Keep the compost damp.

Light Full sun is acceptable only in outdoor cultivation and after exposing the plant gradually to it. Generally, and especially under glass, it is advisable not to give more than 50 per cent sunlight, or 14,000 lx of artificial light.

Temperature *N. alata* lives naturally at high altitudes and therefore in relatively harsh temperatures. Consequently, it is quite happy in rather cooler temperatures of between 10° and 25°C.

Rest Although no natural rest period has been observed, it is advisable to reduce the water supply in winter.

Trimming Well-developed plants can be trimmed periodically (see p.25).

Pests and diseases

The pests most likely to settle on the plants are aphids and red spiders, but even these rarely appear, because the plant's tissues are very tough. Some 19th-century writers recorded thrips on *Nepenthes*. This must be a particularly rare occurrence, since it is nowhere reported in later texts.

Related species

N. alata may be confused with *N. gracilis* or with *N. reinwardtiana*. The main difference is that *N. alata* has a petiole on the leaves; the other two species have not. Also, *N. alata*, unlike the other two species, has a glandular rib under the operculum.

Trap of *N. alata*; the tendril allows it to hook onto a support; × 0.9.

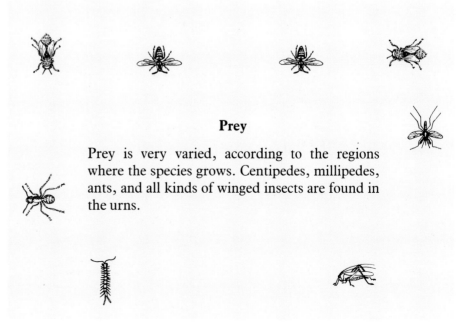

Prey

Prey is very varied, according to the regions where the species grows. Centipedes, millipedes, ants, and all kinds of winged insects are found in the urns.

Passive pitfall trap

Nepenthes villosa

Hairy Nepenthes

Family Nepenthaceae.
Genus The genus *Nepenthes* comprises 72 species living in the wild.
Common name Hairy Nepenthes
Origin Mount Kinabalu in north Borneo.

Size	*prostrate branches*
Exposure	*half shade*
Cultivation	*in pots or hanging baskets*
Humidity	*high*
Temperature	*10° to 25°C*
Flowers	*mostly in summer*
Life span	*indefinite*

Etymology

Villosa is a Latin adjective meaning hairy. The words refers to the numerous fine hairs that cover the entire plant.

Habitat

Nepenthes villosa can be found in mossy, high-altitude forests, between 7800 and 10,000ft (2400 and 3200m).

Description

Dimensions The branches, some ⁵⁄₁₆in (8-9mm) in diameter, bear leaves 4-8½ in (10-22cm) long and 2-3½in (5-9cm) wide. The urn-shaped traps are 4-7in (10-18cm) high and 2-5in (5-12cm) in diameter.
Morphology The leaves, borne on the prostrate branches, have a lance-shaped or oblong limb. On the end nearest the branch they contract into a petiole that surrounds or clasps the branch. Their medial vein extends into a tendril as long, or twice as long, as the limb. Each tendril supports a trap.
Character *N. villosa* is a passive plant: the traps have no movement. Insects drown in them, having been attracted by their nectar glands. They are digested and assimilated by numerous digestive

glands situated at the bottom of the urns. These vary according to their position on the plant. But their peristome is common to them all; this is a very distinctive ring surrounding the mouth of the trap. The peristome on *N. villosa* urns is very wide, as much as ⁷⁄₈in (22mm) for the higher urns, and is provided with large rings ⅛-⁵⁄₁₆in (4-8mm) high. The inside edge of the peristome has teeth that prevent the ensnared prey from climbing out. Like all *Nepenthes*, the urns are surmounted by a lid behind which is a spur or large spine ½in (12mm) long.
Flowers The flowers are grouped into an inflorescence 16-24in (40-60cm) long. Each flower is carried on a stalk and has no petals. The sepals are ⅛in (4mm) long.
Ornamental effect From an ornamental point of view, *N. villosa* is particularly distinctive because of its well-developed ringed peristome and the brown-red hairs with which it is completely covered.
Life span It has an indefinite life span.

Reproduction

Sexual reproduction Obtaining seeds for reproducing the species means cross-fertilizing. (See *Nepenthes alata*: 'Sexual reproduction'.)

Asexual reproduction The usual method of asexual reproduction is to take cuttings. (See *Nepenthes maxima*: 'Asexual reproduction' for details.)

Hybridization

Nepenthes × kinabaluensis is a natural hybrid of *N. rajah* and *N. villosa* – the two species share the same habitat.

Cultivation

Compost See p.23 for the different types of composts that can be used and p.25 for the repotting technique.
Watering Keep the compost constantly damp to ensure that the plants and especially the urns develop well.
Light A supply of light corresponding to 50 per cent of sunlight (about 14,000lx) is sufficient, especially in a greenhouse where too much sun would scorch the foliage.
Temperature *N. villosa* is a high-altitude species, for which temperatures of between 10° and 25°C are suitable. It can even tolerate a temperature as low as 5°C at night.
Rest A reduced amount of water is recommended in winter.
Trimming Page 25 gives the technique.

A *Nepenthes villosa* plant photographed at an altitude of 10,000ft (3000m) in its native region, Mount Kinabalu, on the island of Borneo. The largest urns are so heavy that they touch the ground; × 0.1.

Pests and diseases

Aphids and red spiders may attack cultivated plants. (For treatment, see pp.29 and 30).

Related species

See p.141 for the list of species of the genus *Nepenthes*.

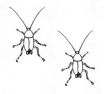

Prey

Invertebrates are relatively rare at altitudes where the plant naturally grows. Nevertheless, it is reasonable to assume that various small creatures living in high-altitude forest are caught – centipedes, millipedes, cockroaches, and ants.

This plate from Curtis's *Botanical Magazine*, 1858, mistakenly describes the plants shown as *Nepenthes veitchii*. It is, in fact, either *N. fusca* or *N. maxima* – the two species are too similar to make identification certain.

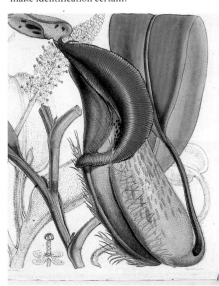

Nepenthes maxima

Passive pitfall trap

Family Nepenthaceae.
Genus The genus *Nepenthes* comprises 72 species living in the wild.
Origin Borneo, Celebes, Moluccas, New Guinea.

	Size	*up to 10ft (3m)*
	Exposure	*half shade*
	Cultivation	*in pots or hanging baskets*
	Humidity	*high*
	Temperature	*10° to 25°C*
	Flowers	*mostly in summer*
	Life span	*indefinite*

Etymology

The specific name, which means largest, is appropriate – the urns or traps can attain a great size.

Habitat

In its natural habitat, *Nepenthes maxima* is found in damp forests at altitudes of between 2000 and 6500ft (600 and 2000m).

Description

Dimensions The sizes of the different organs of *N. maxima* are very variable. The branch, ⅛-⅜in (3-9mm) in diameter, can climb to 10ft (3m). Leaf length can go from 6in (15cm) to 12in (30cm). The urn-shaped traps at the base of the plant are about 8in (20cm) tall; those on the climbing branches may be anything between 3 and 12in (7 and 30cm).

Morphology The creeping branch is cylindrical in section, except at the level of the leaf nodes, where it is triangular. The green leaves are set in various ways on the branches. This diversity, allied to the very variable morphology of the urns, has led many botanists to classify the species under different names, which have now become synonymous.

Character The trap or urn is joined to the plant by a tendril, an extension of the leaf's medial vein. Just like the leaves, the shape and colour of the urns can vary a lot. They go from pure green to an almost black marble. Those at the base curve in towards the tendril but become oval to cylindrical and, higher up, slightly elliptical. Two wings, or expanded membranes, run the length of the traps, which are covered by an oval or almost triangular lid, heart-shaped at the base. The spur, a spine situated at the junction of the lid and the urn, measures ³⁄₁₆in (5mm). The traps on the climbing branches are either cone-shaped or cylindrical. They also have two prominent wings. Whatever the urn's position on the plant, its peristome, the zone that marks the outer edge of the opening, is broad, reaching ¾-1⅞in (20-25mm) in thickness near the lid. The traps are incapable of movement. Insects are first attracted by the nectar glands situated at the level of the peristome. As soon as they go inside the urn, they slip on the smooth inner wall at the top of the trap. They slide down to the bottom, where they are digested by bacteria and numerous glands.

Flowers The flowers are grouped in an inflorescence at least 4in (10cm) long. Neither male nor female flowers have petals. They are colourless, greenish, or brown and exude a fetid odour.

Ornamental effect As with all *Nepenthes*, it is the urns, with their often marbled appearance and wide peristome, that give the plant its character.

Life span Life span is indefinite in good conditions of cultivation.

Reproduction

Sexual reproduction In all *Nepenthes*, the male and female flowers are borne on different plants. Fertilization is achieved by transfering the pollen from a male flower on to the stigma of a female flower (see *Nepenthes alata*: 'Sexual reproduction').

Asexual reproduction The most common method for reproducing *Nepenthes*, and *N. maxima* in particular, is by taking cuttings. This operation must be performed in spring or summer, but the best time is February. The branch must be cut into sections containing three leaves, or possibly four if it is an end cutting (see *Nepenthes albo-marginata*). Treat the cut parts with fungicide and the base of the cutting with growth hormones. The leaves must also be cut back to one third of their length, not forgetting that this cut too must be treated with a fungicide. Use small pots, filled with sphagnum moss or orchid

In *Nepenthes maxima* there are wide differences between the varieties. Variations here are mainly on the urns; × 0.5.

Centre right: taking cuttings from *Nepenthes* is a simple technique that involves cutting the branch into pieces of three or four leaves (1 and 2), then treating and planting them (3). Roots appear after one to three months (4).

compost. It must all kept at temperatures of between 21° and 27°C and under a good light. A root system begins to show after one to three months, at which time the plant should be placed in larger pots, with the usual compost.

Hybridization

Several hybrids of *N. maxima* have been obtained in cultivation (see p.142 for the list of *Nepenthes* hybrids).

Cultivation

Compost Both the composts and the repotting technique are special to *Nepenthes* (see p.23 and p.25 respectively).

Watering/humidity The compost, and if possible the atmosphere around the plant, must be kept constantly very damp.

Light Full sun is only suitable for outdoor cultivation. In a greenhouse, the light must be filtered to create a half shade. In artificial light, use an intensity of about 1,400lx.

Temperature *N. maxima* may be considered a high-altitude species. It can be kept at temperatures of between 10° and 25°C.

Rest Reduce the amount of water slightly in winter.

Trimming Trimming is required for the most vigorous plants (see p.25).

Pests and diseases

Though they are rare, aphids and red spiders can occur, especially on the leaves. (For treatment, see pp.29 and 30.)

Related species

See p.141 for the list of species of the *Nepenthes* genus.

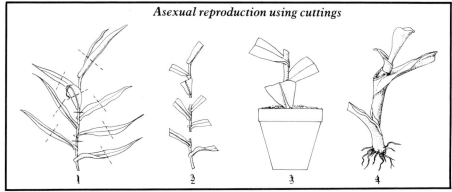

Asexual reproduction using cuttings

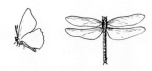

Prey

The large urns that characterize this species occasionally allow large prey to be caught – butterflies, for example. However, most catches are of more modest size.

Nepenthes vieillardii

Passive pitfall trap

New Caledonian Nepenthes

Family Nepenthaceae.
Genus The genus *Nepenthes* comprises 72 species living in the wild.
Common name New Caledonian Nepenthes.
Origin New Caledonia, northwest New Guinea.

	Size	*3ft (1m)*
	Exposure	*half shade*
	Cultivation	*in pots or hanging baskets*
	Humidity	*high*
	Temperature	*10° to 30°C*
	Flowers	*mostly in summer*
	Life span	*indefinite*

Etymology

The specific name honours the French botanist, Eugène Vieillard.

Habitat

Nepenthes vieillardii grows in New Caledonia at altitudes between 300 and 4000ft (100 and 1200m). It has been reported in New Guinea as high as 11,500ft (3500m), an altitude at which there are sharp morning frosts, but this has yet to be confirmed – certainly specimens from New Caledonia that have been subjected to frost have died. In its natural habitat, *N. vieillardii* grows at the foot of bushes, on poor soils, particularly on the most basic substrates, which are the main constituent materials of areas of mining scrub. The species can take the form of a small liana running uncovered along the ground, or grow into dense clumps around bushes; however, on the edges of forests, it can also climb to 50ft (15m) in trees.

The plant is able to survive drought for several months in its original site, but there the morning dew supplies a minimum of water and there is plenty of moisture deep underneath the rock-hard surface of the soil. Daily temperatures are often very high, but nights are always relatively cool.

Description

Dimensions The plant has branches of 3ft (1m) or more in length and of ¼-⁵⁄₁₆in (6-8mm) in diameter. The leaves are 2-8in (5-20cm) long by ⅜-1½in (1-4cm) wide. The urns on the upper part of the plant are larger, reaching 10 in (25cm) in height and some 3in (7-8cm) wide.
Morphology *N. vieillardii* is a robust plant with either erect or climbing branches. The lanceolate leaves are sessile and have two wings at their base. The tendril, an elongation of the medial vein, which carries the trap, is one or one and a half times longer than the limb.
Character In *Nepenthes*, the young urn, at the beginning of its formation, is shaped like a wineskin, closed by a lid and containing a liquid as clear as water or very slightly syrupy. During its development, the lid opens at the front on a fixed hinge. *Nepenthes* traps are passive. The lid overhangs the mouth of the trap, the zone through which insects, attracted by nectar glands, gain access to the trap. Its internal surface is covered with a white powder, is waxy over the upper third, and gives the victims no purchase. They exhaust themselves trying to climb back up the wall. The lower part has three zones covered in a large number of glands. A digestive fluid, secreted by these glands, forms a layer round the bottom of the urn. The glands have the dual function of providing digestive liquid and of absorbing the nutritive substances from the trapped insects. They secrete acids and enzymes, which dissolve the parts that can be assimilated in two or three days. The urns are polymorphous. Those at the base of the plant are rather ovoid near the bottom and cylindrical farther up; they have three fringed wings down their whole length. The urns higher up are cone-shaped. The peristome, a tough edge surrounding the mouth, can be cylindrical or flattened. As with all *Nepenthes*, it has closely packed rings, each one armed with a sharp tooth pointing down inside the trap and preventing victims from escaping. The lid can be spherical or elliptical. Behind its fixed hinge, which links it to the rest of the trap, is a spur ³⁄₁₆-³⁄₁₆in (1-5mm) long.
Flowers The inflorescence is in a bunch; there are numerous flowers, each one borne on a stalk. The sepals, ⅛-³⁄₁₆in (3-5mm) long, can be spherical or elliptical.
Ornamental effect An interesting feature of *N. vieillardii* is its polymorphism; the urns in particular can be very variable in size and colour according to their position on the plant and their exposure to the sun.
Life span The life span is indefinite.

Reproduction

Sexual reproduction In natural conditions, insects fertilize male and female flowers – each on a different plant. Artificially, simply take the pollen from the male flower, using a fine brush, and deposit it on the stigmas of the female flower. The seeds are obtained in four to five months. (See *Nepenthes alata*: 'Sexual reproduction'.)

Asexual reproduction The most common method is to take cuttings. (See *Nepenthes maxima*: 'Asexual reproduction'.)

Cultivation

Compost *N. vieillardii* is a delicate plant and difficult to cultivate; recommended composts are the same as those for all species of the genus (see p.23), as are the precautions to be taken when repotting (see p.25).

Watering Although the species is capable of resisting drought, it will develop well if the compost is kept damp. It is advisable to use rainwater or, failing this, as pure a water as possible.

Light The average intensity of light should be the equivalent of 50 per cent of sunlight, or 14,000lx in artificial light.

Temperature *N. vieillardii*, in natural conditions, grows at various altitudes (see 'Habitat'). It can therefore be cultivated in a range of temperatures between 10° and 30°C. It is able to withstand nocturnal temperatures of 5° and 10°C.

Rest Water less in winter.

Pests and diseases

Aphids may settle on the young leaves or the inflorescences, although attacks are rare. Colonies of red spiders sometimes develop, notably on the leaves. Although certain 19th-century texts noted the possible presence of thrips, small phytophagous insects, on *Nepenthes*, it seems that these are exceptional. (For treatment, see pp.29 and 30.)

Related species

Morphological differences have been noted between those specimens of *N. vieillardii* that are native to New Caledonia and those that come from New Guinea. The latter have more down on their surface and also have a more elliptical operculum, covered with numerous glands on its undersurface.

A population of *Nepenthes vieillardii* on Mount Koghis, in New Caledonia. Depending on the altitude at which it grows, the plant can take on very different forms; here it is in the form of small lianas; × 0.1.

Prey

The prey caught depends more on the area where the plant grows than on its morphological features. All types of insects – above all winged insects – are liable to be captured, from midges to dragonflies.

Nepenthes albo-marginata
Monkey's rice pot

Family Nepenthaceae.
Genus The genus *Nepenthes* comprises 72 species living in the wild.
Common name In Malaysia, monkey's rice pot.
Origin Borneo, Malaysia, Sumatra.

Size	*several metres*
Exposure	*half shade*
Cultivation	*in pots or hanging baskets*
Humidity	*high*
Temperature	*18° to 30°C*
Flowers	*mostly in summer*
Life span	*indefinite*

Etymology

The trap or urn is edged with white below its opening, which explains the specific name.

Habitat

Nepenthes albomarginata grows on rocks at the edge of the sea, among shrubs. It manages to survive on the fine layer of humus that covers these rocks or even on sand. But it also grows over large areas at altitudes up to 4000ft (1200m) and has also been seen on clayey soils.

Description

Dimensions The cylindrical branch is ⅛-¼in (3-7mm) in diameter. The leaves at the base of the plant can be 6in (15cm) long, the intermediate ones up to 12in (30cm), and those situated on the climbing branches 4-10in (10-25cm). The traps or urns can be 5in (12cm) high at the base of the plant and 7½in (19cm) higher up.
Morphology It is a climbing branch. At its base, the leaves are set in an irregular rosette. They are tough, lanceolate, or linear-lanceolate, as are the intermediate leaves. Those situated on the climbing branch are peculiar in having rolled-

Nepenthes albomarginata var. *rubra* in Malaysia. It has a characteristic white band; × 0.4.

under margins and no petiole. The whole of the plant, especially the stem and the young leaves, is covered with fine, russet hair. The leaves are bluish-green.
Character The central leaf vein extends into a tendril, which ends with a trap in the shape of the urn. The tendril, by twisting around a support – for example, a neighbouring plant – can take the weight of the urn. The traps differ in size according to their position on the plant. They are slightly ovoid or nearly cylindrical at their base, cylindrical and cone-shaped near the top. The urn is surmounted by a lid. Two toothed wings or expanded membranes run down the length of the urn. Elsewhere, a sort of

downy ribbon, coloured white and 1/32-1/16in (1-2mm) wide, encircles the top of the urn just under its opening. Digestive glands cover the internal wall of the ovoid part of the urn. They allow the assimilation of prey that has fallen into the digestive liquid at the bottom of the trap. Prey are first attracted by the numerous nectar glands situated on the underside of the lid. Behind this is a large spine or spur. The traps are completely passive.
Flowers The male inflorescence is in a bunch and carried on a floral stem 8-12in (20-30cm) long. The female flowers, also grouped in an inflorescence but 2-10in (5-25cm) long, produce a fruit containing thread-like seeds.
Ornamental effect The plant is distinguishable morphologically by its white-margined urns.
Life span The life span is indefinite if the plant is cultivated under good conditions.

Reproduction

Sexual reproduction Only fertilizing one flower with the pollen from another flower on another plant will give fertile seeds. This cross-pollination, done naturally by insects, must be performed artifically in cultivation. (See *Nepenthes alata*: 'Sexual reproduction'.)

Asexual reproduction One method of reproducing *Nepenthes*, and *N. albomarginata* in particular, is to make a leading-shoot cutting. As for other cuttings, the most favourable time is February. Cut off the end of the branch, along with three or four leaves, and treat the cut parts with fungicide. Growth hormones for cuttings should also be applied to the base of the branch. The leaves on the branch cutting should also be cut back to one third of their length; treat these with fungicide also. Place the cuttings in small pots in sphagnum or orchid compost, keeping them at between 21° and 27°C and under a good light. As soon as a shoot appears at the level of the upper leaf, cut the stem below it, thus obtaining a cutting with one leaf on it. Continue like this for the three or four other leaves of the cutting, each time a new shoot develops.

Hybridization

N. albomarginata is in the parentage of several natural hybrids, including *N. cincta* (*N. albomarginata* × *N. northiana*) and *N. ferrugineo-marginata* (*N. rein-wardtiana* × *N. albomarginata*). Furthermore, *N. masahiroi* (*N. albomarginata* × *N. thorelli*) is a hybrid obtained in cultivation.

Cultivation

Compost See p.23 for the description of all the possible composts and p.25 for the repotting technique.
Watering/humidity The compost must be kept constantly damp and the humid-

ity of the ambient atmosphere maintained at a high 70 per cent.
Light The amount of pigmentation in the ascidia increases as the light intensifies; however, do not exceed an intensity of 50 per cent of sunlight, above all in a greenhouse.
Temperature *N. albomarginata* is considered to be a temperate greenhouse species; it should be cultivated at temperatures of between 18° and 30°C.
Rest Respecting the rest period in win-

A *Nepenthes albomarginata* on Penang Island, Malaysia; × 0.2.

ter means a little less watering.
Trimming Trim any over-developed plants (see p.25).

Pests and diseases

Potentially, the main pests are aphids and red spiders. (For treatment, see pp.29 and 30.)

Related species

See p.141 for the list of species of the genus *Nepenthes*.

Prey

The species grows both on the edge of the sea and at high altitude. Prey likely to be captured is therefore very diverse and varies according to the habitat. Winged insects may be taken – flies, midges, bees, wasps – or small arthropods of all kinds.

Nepenthes ampullaria

Phial Nepenthes

Family Nepenthaceae.
Genus The genus *Nepenthes* comprises 72 species living in the wild.
Common name Phial Nepenthes.
Origin Borneo, Malaysia, New Guinea, Singapore, Sumatra.

	Size	up to 25 ft (8 m)
	Exposure	half shade
	Cultivation	in pots or hanging baskets
	Humidity	high
	Temperature	18° to 30°C
	Flowers	mostly in summer
	Life span	indefinite

Etymology

The specific name derives from the Latin *ampulla*, meaning small flask; it alludes to the rounded and ovoid shape of the ascidia.

Habitat

Nepenthes ampullaria grows by the sea and at altitudes up to 3000ft (1000m), but usually grows between sea level and 300ft (100m). It develops in the swamps of damp forests, on sandy, quartz-based soils, on peaty or clayey ground, but never in salty water. The numerous ascidia are sometimes half shaded and hidden by moss.

Description

Dimensions The stem, ³⁄₁₆-⁵⁄₁₆in (5-8mm) in diameter, can climb up to 25ft (8m). The traps or urns are ¾-4in (2-10cm) high.
Morphology The climbing stem is hard and firm. The base of older plants develops lateral rosettes, comprising numerous urns growing close to each other. Short hairs cover the different parts of the plant, giving it a brown-red tint.
Character The urns forming the traps are basically round, but they narrow at the top and are flattened laterally. Two longitudinal expansions, called wings, ¹⁄₁₆-⁵⁄₁₆in (2-8mm) wide, decorate the exterior wall of the traps, the colour of which may vary from light green to yellow, certain varieties being speckled reddish-purple. The traps are sur-mounted by a wedge-shaped lid, rounded at the apex. Upright when young, the lid later opens outwards so that the urn is no longer protected from the rain. The large spine or spur,

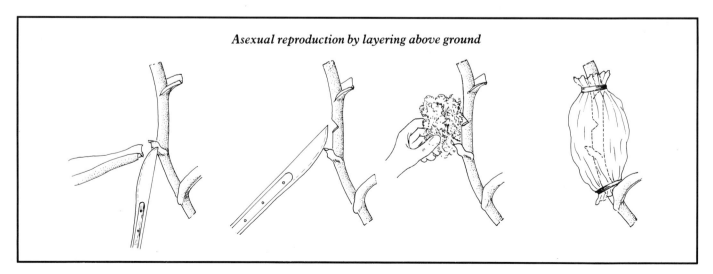

Asexual reproduction by layering above ground

situated behind the lid can be ⅛-⁵⁄₁₆in (3-8mm) long. The digestive glands, which have the dual function of producing the digestive liquid and of absorbing, with the bacteria, the nutritional content of the trapped prey, are very numerous. They line the inner walls at the base of the urns. The traps cannot move.

Flowers The small flowers are grouped in an inflorescence.

Ornamental effect The rosette of urns at the base of older plants gives this plant its distinctive aspect.

Life span The life span is indefinite.

Reproduction

Sexual reproduction As with all *Nepenthes*, the male and female flowers are on different plants; therefore, obtaining seeds means cross-fertilization, either naturally or artificially (see *Nepenthes alata*: 'Sexual reproduction').

Asexual reproduction Layering is one method of asexual reproduction: half cut the branch between two leaves, or cut its outer layers and open them out to make a sort of crown. Treat it with fungicide and place some wet sphagnum over it. Then tie a piece of plastic round it to keep it moist. When the roots begin to form (after about two or three months), cut the branch underneath the newly formed roots and repot the plant in damp compost. Another very common method is to make ordinary cuttings (see *Nepenthes madagascariensis:* 'Asexual reproduction').

Hybridization

N. kuchingensis (*N. ampullaria* × *N. mirabilis*) and *N. trichocarpa* (*N. ampullaria* × *N. gracilis*) are two natural hybrids. In both cases, *N. ampullaria* is the mother plant.

Cultivation

Compost There are many kinds of composts suitable for cultivating *Nepenthes* and *N. ampullaria* in particular (see p.23). However, repotting is a special operation, needing certain precautions (see p.25).

Watering/humidity Both the compost and the surrounding atmosphere should be kept very damp for good development of the urns.

Light An intensity equivalent to 50 per cent of sunlight is sufficient, or about 1,400lx of artificial light. In a green-

The urns of *Nepenthes ampullaria* are surmounted by a small, characteristically shaped operculum; × 0.2.

house, the sun will burn the foliage if the light is not filtered.

Temperature *N. ampullaria* is rather a low-altitude species and should be cultivated at between 18° and 30°C.

Rest Reduce the watering in winter.

Trimming The more vigorous specimens can be pinched back.

Pests and diseases

The pests most likely to trouble *Nepenthes* are aphids and small red spiders. (For treatment, see pp.29 and 30.)

Varieties

One of its many varieties has been introduced into Europe under the name of *N. ampullaria* var. *vittata*, a plant marbled with purple.

Uses

The branches are stiff and very durable – in some countries to which the species is native they are used as ties for making fences. The boiled roots are also used for treating stomach ailments.

Prey

The prey is invertebrates living in damp regions – insects, myriapods, and other small arthropods.

Passive pitfall trap

Nepenthes bicalcarata

Twin-spurred Nepenthes

Family Nepenthaceae
Genus The genus *Nepenthes* comprises 72 species living in the wild.
Common name Twin-spurred Nepenthes.
Origin Northwest Borneo.

	Size	up to 50ft (15m)
	Exposure	half shade
	Cultivation	in pots or hanging baskets
	Humidity	high
	Temperature	18° to 30°C
	Flowers	mostly in summer
	Life span	indefinite

Etymology

The word *bicalcarata* means with two spurs. It refers to a morphological peculiarity of the species – there are two curved spines at the top, pointing down into the trap.

Habitat

Nepenthes bicalcarata grows in damp forests and other swampy areas, at altitudes between sea level and 3000ft (950m).

Description

Dimensions The stem reaches a maximum height of 50ft (15m) and has a diameter of between ¼-⁹⁄₁₆in (6-15mm). The leaves are 8-24in (20-60cm) long and 2¼-4¾in (6-12cm) wide. The traps are between 2-5in (5-13cm) high.
Morphology The cylindrical, climbing branches bear tough, petioled leaves, obovate and lanceolate; they are dark green on the upper surface and light green underneath. The petiole, which has two wings or membranous expansions, forms a sheath around the branch. As with all species of *Nepenthes*, the medial vein extends into a tendril, which carries the trap. In *N. bicalcarata* this

tendril measures 4-12in (10-30cm); its diameter increases nearer the trap. Shoots can appear around older traps.
Character The urn-shaped traps are of different sizes according to their position on the plant. Those at the base are as high as they are wide, and rounded. Two wings, ¼-½in (6-12mm) wide and lined with ¹⁄₃₂-³⁄₁₆in (1-5mm) hairs, run the length of the trap. Each trap is surmounted by a lid, uniform and raised on a neck ¾-1¼in (2-3cm) high. The lid is fixed – *Nepenthes* traps are passive. Underneath the lid are the two spines that give the species its name. It has been suggested that these two spines prevent the urns being damaged by monkeys. The traps of the upper leaves are longer than the others. Whatever their position, all urns have, as well as the two spines already mentioned, a spur at the back of the lid pointing outwards. The traps are rust-red colour on the outside and light green on the inside; the edge of the opening, or peristome, is also light green. Insects are attracted by the numerous orbicular nectar glands on the lid. When they enter the trap, they find no foothold on the white-dusted, waxy wall; they fall to the bottom where numerous microscopic glands, together with bacteria, help to assimilate them.
Flowers The flowers are grouped in an inflorescence.

The urn of a young *Nepenthes bicalcarata* plant; the two spines pointing inside the trap and situated under the operculum give it its name; × 1.5.

Ornamental effect The shape of the trap and the unusual nature of the lid give this plant its ornamental value.
Life span Its life span is indefinite.

Reproduction

Sexual reproduction Seeds can be obtained by fertilizing a female flower with a male flower, which are always on different plants (see *Nepenthes alata*: 'Sexual reproduction').

Asexual reproduction Besides taking cuttings (see *Nepenthes madagascariensis*: 'Asexual reproduction'), one method of reproducing *N. bicalcarata* consists of layering; choose a section of branch between two leaves and make an incision to half its diameter. Treat it with fungicide and bend the branch over and place the cut part into a seed tray or pot filled with sphagnum or other compost. When roots have developed, cut the branch to separate the layer from the mother plant.

Cultivation

Compost Like other species of the genus, *N. bicalcarata* can be cultivated in a variety of composts (see p.23); remember to repot those plants that become too large for their containers (see p.25).

Watering Rainwater is best for the plant. Water constantly.

Light *Nepenthes* in general, and *N. bicalcarata* in particular, are plants which prefer half shade. In artificial light, supply an intensity of 1,400lx.

Temperature *N. bicalcarata* in its native habitat is a low-altitude plant; in cultivation it must be kept at high temperatures, between about 18° and 30°C.

Rest No changes in cultivation conditions are necessary in winter, except for a slight reduction in the amount of water.

Trimming This may be required for well-developed specimens (see p.25).

An elongated urn at the top of a plant. The two small spines under the operculum are easily visible; × 0.5.

An urn at the base of a plant, characterized by its squat shape; × 0.5.

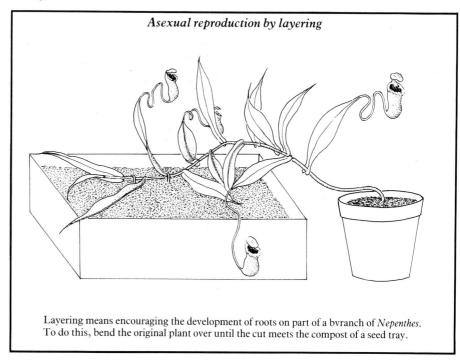

Asexual reproduction by layering

Layering means encouraging the development of roots on part of a bvranch of *Nepenthes*. To do this, bend the original plant over until the cut meets the compost of a seed tray.

Prey

In the plant's natural habitat, invertebrates from damp areas are normally caught. The traps on the climbing branches capture winged insects in particular.

Pests and diseases

Because of the toughness of their leaves, *Nepenthes* are rarely attacked by pests. This is why aphids are found only on the young leaves. (For treatment, see p.29.)

Related species

See p.141 for the list of species of the genus *Nepenthes*.

Passive pitfall trap

Nepenthes madagascariensis

Madagascan Nepenthes

Family Nepenthaceae.
Genus The genus *Nepenthes* comprises 72 species living in the wild.
Common name Madagascan Nepenthes.
Origin East coast of Madagascar (from Toamasina to Faradofay).

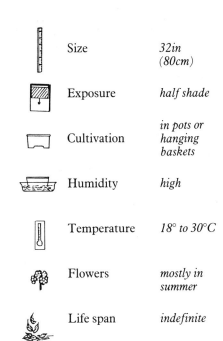

	Size	*32in (80cm)*
	Exposure	*half shade*
	Cultivation	*in pots or hanging baskets*
	Humidity	*high*
	Temperature	*18° to 30°C*
	Flowers	*mostly in summer*
	Life span	*indefinite*

History and etymology

Nepenthes madagascariensis was described in 1796 by the French naturalist Jean Louis Marie Poiret, a colleague of Lamarck. The species had been discovered in 1658 by E. de Falcourt, governor of Madagascar, but the samples he examined came from herbaria and he was unaware of the liquid in the ascidia that is responsible for digesting prey. The species is endemic to Madagascar, hence its name.

Habitat

The Madagascan Nepenthes grows on open ground, scattered with bushes; the substrate can be sandy or heathland.

Description

Dimensions On average, the plant reaches 32in (80cm) in height and the leaves are 10in (25cm) long.
Morphology *N. madagascariensis* is rarely a creeper; it forms bush-like tufts. The straight stem bears oblong leaves, narrowing at the base into a grooved petiole. The tendril extending from it is shorter than the leaf. It is arched and, when young, covered in russet hair. Like other species of *Nepenthes*, it carries an urn at its extremity.

Upper part of an urn of *N. madagascariensis*. The nectar glands under the operculum are clearly visible; ×1.5.

Character There are numerous traps or urns. Those at the base of the plant are bulbous over the lower third and narrow at the top. On the outside they have two longitudinal, fimbriate wings. The mouth or opening is almost circular. It is surmounted by a lid, which is kidney-shaped and arched. The traps are reddish or bright red. All the traps are passive : insects, attracted by the nectar glands of the lid and peristome, fall into a digestive liquid secreted by glands covering the bottom of the trap.

Flowers The flowers grow in an inflorescence.
Ornamental effect The bush-like shape of *N. madagascariensis* distinguishes it morphologically from the many other species of Nepenthes that are climbers.
Life span In good conditions of culture life span is indefinite.

Reproduction

Sexual reproduction Pollen must be transferred from the male flower to the female flower, which are always on different plants, as with all *Nepenthes* (see *Nepenthes alata* : 'Sexual reproduction').
Asexual reproduction Taking cuttings is a very common method of asexual reproduction; if possible, it should be done in February, in any case in spring or, failing this, in summer. It involves first cutting the branch into sections of three leaves. All the cut parts must be treated with fungicide and, also, growth hormones must be applied to the base of the cuts. The leaves should be cut to a third of their length and treated with fungicide. The prepared cuttings are placed in small pots containing orchid composts or simply sphagnum. The temperature should be kept between 21° and 27°C. After one to three months, when the roots have developed, repot into a *Nepenthes* compost (see p.23 for

the compost formulae for cultivating *Nepenthes*).

Cultivation

Compost *N. madagascariensis* is difficult to transplant and to raise. (See p.23 for the compost formulae for *Nepenthes* and p.25 for the repotting technique.)

Watering The compost must be kept constantly damp for the plants to develop well.

Light An intensity corresponding to 50 per cent of sunlight is sufficient in a greenhouse, where unfiltered light from the sun would scorch the plants.

Temperature. *N. madagascariensis* is a low-altitude species, for cultivation purposes, it must be considered a hothouse plant and kept at temperatures of between 18° and 30°C.

Rest There is no proper rest period. Simply reduce the amount of water in winter.

Trimming Trim plants that become overgrown (see p.25).

Pests and diseases

Aphids and red spiders may settle on the plants. (For treatment see pp.29 and 30.)

Related species

N. masoalensis, also native to Madagascar, is a plant whose urns at the base of the stem are similiar to those of the Madagascan Nepenthes. It grows naturally, often on humus, in the northeast of the Masoala peninsula, a region that is especially hot and humid. It is difficult to cultivate.

N. masoalensis, a species related to *N. madagascriensis* that also is found in Madagascar; × 0.3.

Uses

The naturalist Poiret described the properties of this species in the *Encyclopédie Méthodique*: 'The root of this plant is reputedly astringent and the leaves moist and refreshing. A distillate made from the plant is swallowed to reduce high fevers and applied to the skin to combat inflammations, erysipelas, etc.'

Prey

There are many traps on this plant and the prey taken is numerous and varied – ants and all kinds of winged insects, midges, flies, bees, wasps, etc.

Nepenthes rafflesiana

Raffles' Nepenthes

Family Nepenthaceae.
Genus The genus *Nepenthes* comprises 72 species living in the wild.
Common name Raffles' Nepenthes.
Origin Borneo, Malaysia, Singapore, Sumatra.

	Size	*up to 50ft (15m)*
	Exposure	*half shade*
	Cultivation	*in pots or hanging baskets*
	Humidity	*high*
	Temperature	*18° to 30°C*
	Flowers	*mostly in summer*
	Life span	*indefinite*

Etymology

The species is dedicated to Sir Stamford Raffles, the founder of Singapore.

Habitat

Nepenthes rafflesiana usually grows in the open on damp or swampy ground, frequently on the edges of forests or even among ferns. The highest altitude at which it has been found is 4600ft (1395m).

Description

Dimensions The stem often reaches a length of 13ft (4m), or more rarely 50ft (15m), and has a diameter of ⅛-⁵/₁₆in (4-8mm). The leaves are 4-14in (10-35cm) long and 2-4in (5-10cm) wide. The urn-shaped traps are of variable dimensions. Those at the base are 10in (25cm) tall at most and 5in (12cm) wide, while those higher up are longer and can reach 12in (30cm) tall by 4in (10cm) wide.
Morphology The climbing branch has elliptical leaves. The limb narrows towards the branch into a petiole having two wings or membranous expansions.
Character The urns are borne by a tendril, which is an extension of the central leaf vein. They contain a diges-

tive liquid in which insects drown. The morphology, as well as the size of the urns, changes according to their position on the plant. At the base of the plant the urns are rounded at the bottom and conical at the top. They have two, wide, longitudinal wings arising from the tendril; this feature is specific to *Nepenthes rafflesiana*. The peristome or trap opening is surmounted by a spherical lid, supported by a fixed hinge; behind this is a large spine or spur ¾in (20mm) long. The upper urns are cone-shaped and longer than the lower ones. Whatever their position on the plant, the urns have numerous digestive glands on their inner wall. They are green or light green in colour and spotted with varying shades of purple or red. They are passive traps and do not move.
Flowers The inflorescence, in a bunch, is 6-20in (15-50cm) long. Each flower is borne by a small pedicel.
Ornamental effect The species is interesting in the shape of its traps and also in the varieties that come from it.
Life span The life span is indefinite, like all species of the genus.

Reproduction

Sexual reproduction Any one flower cannot fertilize itself since it is either male or female. In nature pollination of one flower by another is ensured by insects. To obtain seeds in cultivation it is necessary to fertilize artificially (see *Nepenthes alata*: 'Sexual reproduction').
Asexual reproduction One technique for asexual reproduction consists of air layering; half cut the branch between two leaves, or cut the outside tissues of the branch to make a sort of crown. Treat the exposed parts with fungicide and place damp sphagnum around the incision. Cover it all with a sheet of plastic in order to keep it damp. When a root has developed (after two to three months), cut the branch under the root and repot it in the normal compost, always keeping it damp. Another very common method is to take cuttings (see *Nepenthes madagascariensis* : 'Asexual reproduction').

Hybridization

N. hookeriana is a natural hybrid from a cross between *N. ampullaria* (the mother plant) and *N. rafflesiana*. Many other hybrids have been obtained in cultivation from *N. rafflesiana* (see p.142 for the list of *Nepenthes* hybrids).

Nepenthes rafflesiana : a plant on display at a floral exhibition, amongst other exotic species. The urns, hanging at the ends of the leaves, are spotted with red; × 0.2

Cultivation

Compost *N. rafflesiana*, like other species of the same genus, can be cultivated in a variety of composts (see p.23). Repotting is a relatively delicate operation (see p.25).

Watering/humidity To ensure good plant development keep both the compost and the surrounding air constantly damp.

Light Lighting must be the equivalent of 50 per cent sunlight. Under glass the sun must be filtered to avoid scorching.

Temperature In its natural environment, *N. rafflesiana* is a low-altitude plant; the species should therefore be maintained at between 18° and 30°C.

Rest Simply reduce the water a little in winter.

Trimming The most vigorous plants can be staked to support them (see p.25).

Pests and diseases

Aphids and red spiders do occasionally settle on *Nepenthes*. (For treatment see pp.29 and 30.)

Varieties

N. rafflesiana can occur in a number of varieties. *N. rafflesiana* var. *elongata* has leaves and traps twice as big as those of the species type, while *N. rafflesiana* var. *minor* is much smaller. Finally, *N. rafflesiana* var. *nigro-purpurea* and *N. rafflesiana* var. *punctata* can be distinguished by the colour of their urns, those of the first being purple-brown and those of the second displaying many reddish-brown spots.

Prey

The main catch of the traps on the climbing branches is winged insects, from the size of a midge to that of a dragonfly or butterfly.

137

Species and hybrids

Below (pp.138 to 142) is a list of the principal species of carnivorous plants and their hybrids.

The name of a species studied in detail in the book is in **bold** type; it is followed by the number of the page at which the species is discussed. Plants that are only mentioned or illustrated in the book are in Roman type.

For the cultivation of species not covered in this book, please refer to the detailed descriptions of plants which appear in the same list and which therefore have similar cultivation requirements.

In the lists of hybrids (genera *Drosera*, *Sarracenia*, and *Nepenthes*), the sign × indicates that these plants come from a cross between species or hybrids. In the name of the parentage, the seed-bearing or mother plant is cited first.

Sole species of their genus

Aldrovanda vesiculosa (p. 54)
Byblis liniflora et *Byblis gigantea* (p. 86)
Cephalotus follicularis (p. 43; p. 114)
Darlingtonia californica (p. 39; p. 92)
Dionaea muscipula (pp. 33 et 34; p. 50)
Drosophylum lusitanicum (p. 90)

Principal species of *Drosera* from temperate climates

NAME	REGION OF ORIGIN	BIOLOGICAL AND CULTIVATION CHARACTERISTICS
D. aliciae	South Africa	C, O
D. anglica (p. 71)	Europe	I, N, O
D. arcturi	New Zealand	I
D. binata (p. 36; p. 64)	Australia	I, C
D. brevifolia	USA	L, C, O
D. burkeana	South Africa	C, O
D. burmannii	Australia, Asia	L, O
D. capensis (pp. 35 et 46; p. 66)	South Africa	C, O
D. capillaris	USA	C, O
D. cistiflora	South Africa	T, S, O
D. corsica	Corsica	I, N, O
D. cuneifolia	South Africa	C, O
D. filiformis (p. 68)	USA	I, N, O
D. glabripes	South Africa	C
D. glanduligera	Australia	L, O
D. hamiltonii	Australia	C
D. intermedia (p. 69)	Europe	I, N, O
D. linearis	USA, Canada	I, N, O
D. montana	Brazil, Venezuela	C, O
D. natalensis	South Africa	C, O
D. peltata	Australia, Asia, Japan	T, S, O
D. ramellosa	Australia	T, S, O
D. regia	South Africa	C
D. rotundifolia (p. 70)	Europe, Canada, USA	I, N, O
D. spathulata	Asia, New Zealand, etc	C, O
D. stenopetala	New Zealand	C, O
D. trinervia	South Africa	C
D. villosa	Brazil	C
D. whittakeri	Australia	T

Some *Drosera* hybrids from temperate climates

NAME	PARENTS	BIOLOGICAL AND CULTIVATION CHARACTERISTICS
D × *hybrida* (p. 69)	(*D. filiformis* × *D. intermedia*)	I, N
D. × *nagamoto*	(*D. anglica* × *D. spathulata*)	I, C
D. × *obovata* (p. 71)	(*D. anglica* × *D. rotundifolia*)	I, N

Species of *Drosera* from tropical climates

NAME	REGION OF ORIGIN	BIOLOGICAL AND CULTIVATION CHARACTERISTICS
D. adelae	Australia	V
D. affinis	Tropical Africa	O
D. burkeana	South Africa	V, O
D. burmannii	Australia, Asia	V, L, O
D. indica	Tropical regions	L
D. madagascariensis	Madagascar	L
D. neo-caledonica	New Caledonia	L
D. petiolaris	Australia	V
D. prolifera	Australia	V
D. schizandra	Australia	V, O
D. spathulata (p. 72)	Australia, Asia	V, O

Notes *on the* Drosera *from temperate and tropical climates:*
1. For the *Drosera* from tropical climates, self-fertilization is mentioned only for those species where we have been able to verify the phenomenon experimentally.
2. Certain species figure in both the temperate and tropical-climate lists. This means that they can be kept in continual growth (without a rest period) or be given a yearly rest.

Species of pygmy *Drosera* described

D. androsacea	*D. omissa*
D. barbigera	*D. paleacea*
syn. *drummondii*	*D. platystigma*
D. glanduligera	*D. pulchella* U
D. leucoblasta	*D. pycnoblasta*
D. miniata	**D. pygmaea** U (p. 76)
D. nitidula	*D. scorpioides*
D. occidentalis	*D. sewelliae*

Species of pygmy *Drosera* not yet described

D. bannister U	*D. muchea* U
D. brookton	*D. north beermullah* U
D. lake badgerup (p. 77) U	*D. regans ford*
D. millbrook road	*D. toodyay*
D. mount manypeak	*D. walyinga*

Note: *origin of the pygmy* Drosera
1. All species of pygmy *Drosera* are natives of Australia, Tasmania, or New Zealand, the majority being Australian. Species not yet described bear the name of the place where they were discovered.

Principal species of tuberous *Drosera*

NAME	BOTANICAL CHARACTERISTICS	NAME	BOTANICAL CHARACTERISTICS
D. andersoniana (p. 75)	D	*D. microphylla*	D
D. auriculata (p. 36)	D	*D. modesta* (p. 46)	D, P
D. bulbigena	D	*D. myriantha*	D
D. bulbosa	R	*D. neesii*	D
D. erythrorhiza	R	*D. orbiculata*	R
D. fimbriata	D	*D. pallida*	D, P
D. gigantea	D	**D. peltata** (p. 74)	D
D. graniticola	D	*D. platypoda*	D
D. heterophylla	D	*D. radicans*	D
D. huegelii	D	*D. ramellosa*	D
D. lowriei	R	*D. rosulata*	R
D. macrantha	D, P	*D. salina*	D
D. macrophylla (pp. 37 and 46)	R	*D. stolonifera*	D
		D. stricticaulis	D
D. marchantii (p. 36)	D	*D. subhirtella*	D, P
D. menziesii	D, P	*D. tubaestylus*	R
		D. zonaria	R

Note: *origin of the tuberous* Drosera
All these species are natives of Australia. *D. auriculata* is also found in New Zealand; *D. peltata* also comes from Asia, China, India, and Japan.

Key: *biological and cultivation characteristics of the* Drosera

L = Annual plant
I = Plant that transforms into a hibernaculum in winter
T = Plant having a tuber or underground rhizome
C = Continuous foliage throughout winter above +7°C, the plant withers below 7°C
N = Plant unable to withstand frost
S = Plant resting (dry) in summer
O = Self-fertilizing flowers
V = Continuous growth
U = Species living in constant damp
R = Plant with rosettes of leaves
D = Erect plant or one with a well-developed stem
P = Climbing or creeping plant

Principal species of *Pinguicula* from temperate climates

NAME	REGION OF ORIGIN	BIOLOGICAL AND CULTIVATION CHARACTERISTICS
P. alpina	Europe	A, K, I
P. balcanica	Greece, Yugoslavia	A, K, I
P. corsica	Corsica	A, I
P. grandiflora	Europe	A, K, I
P. leptoceras	Alps	A, K, I
P. longifolia	Europe	K, I
P. macroceras	North America, Japan, Russia	A, K, I
P. nevadensis	Spain	A, I
P. ramosa	Japan	A, I
P. vallisneriifolia	Spain	K, I
P. variegata	Siberia	A, I
P. villosa	North America, Asia, arctic and antarctic regions of Europe	A, I
P. vulgaris (p. 78)	North America, Europe, Siberia	A, K, I

Principal species of *Pinguicula* from warm or semi-tropical climates

NAME	REGION OF ORIGIN	BIOLOGICAL AND CULTIVATION CHARACTERISTICS
P. caerulea (p. 47)	USA	A
P. moranensis (p. 38; **p. 82**) (= *P. caudata*)	Mexico	A, K
P. colimensis	Mexico	A, K
P. cyclosecta	Mexico	A, K
P. gypsicola	Mexico	A, K
P. hirtiflora	Southern Italy	A
P. ionantha	USA	A
P. lilacina	Mexico	A
P. lusitanica	North Africa, Western Europe	A, I
P. lutea (p. 47; **p. 84**)	USA	A
P. macrophylla	Mexico	A, K, I
P. oblongiloba	Mexico	A, K, I
P. planifolia	USA	A
P. primuliflora	USA	A
P. pumila	USA	A

Key: *biological and cultivation characteristics of* Pinguicula
A = Species from an acid soil
K = Species from an alkaline soil
I = Species that transforms into a hibernaculum in winter

Species of the genus *Heliamphora*

H. heterodoxa (pp. 98 and 99)
H. ionasi (p. 99)
H. minor (pp. 39, 97, 98 and 99)
H. neblinae (p. 99)
H. nutans (p. 96)
H. tatei (p. 99)

Principal species of the genus *Utricularia*

NAME	REGION OF ORIGIN	BIOLOGICAL AND CULTIVATION CHARACTERISTICS
U. alpina (p. 47; **p. 62**) (= *U. montana*)	Antilles, Central and South America	E, M'
U. amethystina	North America, Trinidad	V, M'
U. aurea	Red China	Q, M'
U. australis (= U. neglecta)	Australia, Europe, Africa, Japan, Asia, New Zealand	Q, F, G, I
U. biflora	USA	Q, F
U. caerulea	India	V, M'
U. calycifida	Venezuela, Guyana	V, M
U. campbelliana	Venezuela, Guyana	E, M'
U. capensis	South Africa	V, M'
U. cornuta	USA	V, F, G
U. delicatula	New Zealand	V, M
U. dichotoma (p. 34)	Australia, Tasmania	V, M'
U. dusenii	South America	V, M
U. endresii	Antilles, Costa Rica	E, M'
U. exoleta	Australia, Asia, Africa, Europe (Spain and Portugal)	Q, F
U. fibrosa	USA	Q, F, G, I
U. floridana	USA	Q, F
U. foliosa	USA	Q, F
U. geminiscapa	USA	Q, F, G, I
U. gibba	Africa, Antilles, Asia, USA	Q, F, G, I
U. hookeri	Australia	Q, M'
U. humboldtii	Venezuela	E, M'
U. hydrocarpa	USA	Q, M
U. ianthina	Brazil	E
U. inflata	USA	Q, F, G, I
U. intermedia	Asia, USA, Europe	Q, F, G, I
U. jamesoniana	Central and South America	E, M
U. juncea	USA	V, G
U. laterifolia	Australia, Tasmania	V, M'
U. leptoplectra	Australia	V, M
U. lloydii	South America	V, M
U. livida	South Africa	V, M
U. longifolia	South America (Brazil)	E, M
U. macrorhiza	USA	Q, F, G, I
U. menziesii	Australia	V, M, M', I
U. minor	Asia, USA, Europe	Q, F, G, I
U. monanthos	New Zealand	V, M'
U. nelumbifolia	Brazil	E, M'
U. nephrophylla	Brazil	E, M'
U. nova-zelandiae	New Zealand	V, M'
U. obtusa	Brazil	Q, M
U. ochroleuca	Europe, USA	Q, F, G, I
U. olivacea	USA	Q, F
U. praelonga	South America	V, M
U. praetermissa	Colombia, Costa Rica, Nicaragua, Panama	E, M
U. prehensilis	tropical Africa	V, M
U. purpurea	Canada, Cuba, USA	Q, F, G, I
U. quelchii	Guyana, Venezuela	E, M, M'
U. racemosa	Asia	V, M
U. radiata	USA	Q, F, G, I
U. reniformis	Brazil, Guyana Venezuela	E, M, M'
U. resupinata	USA	V, F, G, I
U. reticulata	Asia	V
U. sandersonii (p. 60)	South Africa	V, M'
U. scandens	India	V, M
U. simulans (= U. fimbriata)	USA	V, M', F
U. spiralis	Africa	V, M
U. stellaris (= U. inflexa)	Africa, Asia, Australia	Q, M'

NAME	REGION OF ORIGIN	BIOLOGICAL AND CULTIVATION CHARACTERISTICS
U. subulata	Africa, America, Borneo, Madagascar, Portugal, Thailand	V, M
U. tricolor	South America	V, M
U. uliginosa	Asia	V, M
U. unifolia	South America	E, M
U. violacea	Australia	V, M'
U. volubilis	Southwestern Australia	Q
U. vulgaris (p. 56)	Africa, Asia, Australia, Europe, Japan, New Zealand	Q, F, G, I

Key: *the biological and cultural characteristics of* Utricularia

Q = Aquatic plant
V = Terrestrial plant
E = Epiphytic plant
M = Tropical plant (temperatures of 17° to 36°C on average in summer and 9° to 21°C in winter)
M' = Subtropical plant (temperatures of 16° to 30°C on average in summer and 6° to 18°C in winter)
F = Temperate climate plant (temperatures of 15° to 30°C on average in summer and 3° to 14°C in winter)
G = Withstands frost (temperatures of 12° to 28°C on average in summer and 0° to 7°C in winter)
I = Plant that transforms into a hibernaculum at temperatures below +7°C.

Species of the genus *Sarracenia*

S. alata	S. oreophila
S. flava (p. 100)	**S. psittacina** (p. 108)
S. leucophylla (p. 104)	**S. purpurea** (p. 47, **p. 110**)
S. minor (p. 41; **p. 106**)	S. rubra (p. 47)

Principal registered hybrids of *Sarracenia*

NAME	PARENTS	SYNONYMS
S. × ahlsii	alata × rubra	
S. × areolata	leucophylla × alata	
S. × cantabrigiensis	leucophylla × minor	S. × excellens
S. × caroli-schmidti	chelsonii × purpurea	
S. × catesbaei (pp. 41 and 47)	flava × purpurea	S. × stevensii S. × williamsii
S. × chelsonii	purpurea × rubra	
S. × courtii	purpurea × psittacina	
S. × crispata	flava × minor	S. × harperi
S. × decora	psittacina × minor	
S. × exornata	alata × purpurea	S.×cantabrigiensis
S. × farnhamii	leucophylla × rubra	
S. × flambeau	purpurea × minor	S. × swaniana
S. × formosa	minor × psittacina	S.×maddisoniana
S. × gilpini	rubra × psittacina	S. × crispata
S. × illustrata	flava × catesbaei	
S. × kaufmanniana	chelsonii × purpurea	
S. × melanorhoda	catesbaei × purpurea	
S. × mitchelliana	leucophylla × purpurea	
S. × mooreana	leucophylla × flava	S. × mandaiana
S. × popei	flava × rubra	
S. × readi	leucophylla × rubra	
S. × rehderi	rubra × minor	
S. × sanderana	leucophylla × farnhamii	
S. × vittata	purpurea × chelsonii	
S. × willisii	courtii × melanorhoda	
S. × wrigleyana	leucophylla × psittacina	

Principal species of the genus *Nepenthes*

NAME	REGION OF ORIGIN	ALTITUDE
N. alata (p. 118) (*blancoi; copelandii, eustachys; gracili-flora; phyllamphora*)	BO., MA., MO., PH., SU.	H
N. albomarginata (p. 128) (*teysmanniana*)	BO., MA., SU.	B
N. ampullaria (p. 130)	BO., MA., NG., SU.	B
N. annamensis	VN.	H
N. bellii	PH.	B
N. bicalcarata (p.132)	BO.	B
N. bongso	SU.	H
N. boschiana	BO.	H
N. burbidgeae	BO.	H
N. campanulata	BO.	B
N. carunculata	SU.	H
N. clipeata	BO.	H
N. deaniana	PH.	H
N. decurrens	BO.	B
N. densiflora	SU.	H
N. dentata	CE.	H
N. distillatoria (*zeylanica*)	Sri Lanka	H
N. dubia	SU.	H
N. edwardsiana	BO.	H
N. ephippiata	BO.	H
N. fusca	BO.	H
N. geoffrayi	VN.	H
N. globamphora	PH.	B
N. gracilis (pp. 45 and 121) (*angustifolia; laevis*)	BO., CE., MA., SU.	B
N. gracillima (*ramispina*)	MA.	H
N. gymnamphora (*melamphora*)	J., SU., BO.	H
N. hirsuta (*hispida*)	BO.	H
N. inermis	SU.	H
N. insignis	NG.	B
N. kampotiana (p. 48)	VN.	B
N. khasiana	India (Mount Khasia)	H
N. klossii	NG.	H
N. leptochila	BO.	H
N. lowii	BO.	H
N. macfarlanei	MA.	H
N. madagascariensis (p. 134)	Madagascar	B
N. masoalensis (p. 135)	Madagascar	B
N. maxima (p. 124) (*celebica; curtisii*)	BO., CE., MO., NG.	H
N. merrilliana (*surigaoensis*)	CE., PH.	B
N. mirabilis (*albo-lineata; alicae; armbrustae; beccari; bernaysii, cholmondeleyi; echinostoma; garrawayae; jardinei; kekkediana; moorei; phyllamphora; rowanae; smilesii; tubulosa*)	AU., BO., China, J., MA., NG., PH., SU., VN.	B
N. mollis	BO.	H
N. muluensis	BO.	H
N. neglecta	BO.	B
N. neoguineensis	NG.	B
N. northiana (*spuria*)	BO.	B
N. paniculata	NG.	H
N. papuana	NG.	B
N. pectinata	SU.	H
N. pervillei	Seychelles	H
N. petiolata	PH.	B
N. pilosa	BO.	H
N. rafflesiana (p. 42; p. 136) (*hemsleyana*)	BO., MA., SU.	B
N. rajah	B.	H
N. reinwardtiana (p. 121)	BO., MA., MO., SU.	B
N. rhombicaulis	SU.	H
N. sanguinea (*pumila*) (p. 45)	MA.	H
N. singalana	SU.	H
N. spathulata	SU.	H
N. spectabilis	SU.	H

NAME	REGION OF ORIGIN	ALTITUDE
N. stenophylla (*fallax*)	BO.	H
N. tentaculata	BO., CE.	H
N. thorellii	VN.	B
N. tobaica	SU.	H
N. tomoriana	CE.	B
N. treubiana	NG., SU.	H
N. truncata	PH.	B
N. ventricosa (p. 44)	PH.	H
N. vieillardii (*montrouzieri*) (p. 126)	NC., NG.	B
N. villosa (*harryana*) (p. 122).	BO.	H

Key: *native sites of* Nepenthes

1) **Countries of origin:**
AU: Australia; BO: Borneo; CE: Celebes; J: Java; MA: Malaysia; MO: Maluku; NC: New Caledonia; NG: New Guinea; PH: Philippines; SU: Sumatra; VN: Vietnam.

2) **Altitudes of growth:**
H = Species living naturally at an altitude above 3250ft (1000m) ('high altitude')
B = Species living naturally at an altitude below 3250ft (1000m) ('low altitude')

Note: *nomenclature of* Nepenthes
The names in brackets are regarded as synonymous with the preceding name of the plant; the first name given is the recognized one, which must be retained.

Natural hybrids of *Nepenthes*

NAME	PARENTS
N. × cincta (p. 123)	*albo-marginata × northiana*
N. × ferrugineo-marginata (p. 129)	*reinwardtiana × albomarginata*
N. × hookeriana (p. 136)	*ampullaria × rafflesiana*
N. × junghuhnii	*sanguinea × singalana*
N. ×kinabaluensis (p. 122)	*rajah × villosa*
N. × kuchingensis (p. 130)	*ampullaria × mirabilis*
N. × lecouflei	*mirabilis × thorellii*
N. × merrilliata (p. 120)	*alata × merrilliana*
N. × trasmadiensis	*edwardsiana × lowii*
N. × trichocarpa (p. 130)	*ampullaria × gracilis*
N. × ventrata (p. 120)	*alata × ventricosa*

Table p. 142: hybrids of *Nepenthes* obtained in cultivation. ▶

Hybrids of *Nepenthes* obtained in cultivation

Name	Parents	Name	Parents
N. × accentual koto	thorelii × hookerania	N. × kikuchiae	oiso × maxima
N. × aichi	thorelii × balfouriana	N. × koiso	neufvilliana × ladenburgii
N. × aigae	oiso × thorelii	N. × krausii	mixta × tiveyi
N. × allardii	veitchii × maxima	N. × ladenburgii	mixta × maxima
N. × alliotii	northiana × maxima	N. × lawrenciana	mirabilis × hookeriana
N. × amabilis	hookeriana × rafflesiana	N. × longicaudata	maxima superba × northiana
N. × ambrosial koto	trichocarpa × hookeriana	N. × lyrata	hybrida × rafflesiana
N. × amesiana	rafflesiana × hookeriana	N. × maria louisa	= mixta (northiana × maxima)
N. × arakawae	mixta × alata	N. × masahiroi (p. 129)	albomarginata × thorelii
N. × atropurpurea	sanguinea × maxima superba	N. × masamiae	thorelii × maxima
N. × atrosanguinea	distillatoria × sedenii	N. × mastersiana	sanguinea × khasiana
N. × balfouriana	mixta × mastersiana	N. × mercieri	northiana × maxima
N. × balmy koto	thorelii × maxima	N. × minamiensis	oiso × wrigleyana
N. × bohnickii	mixta × maxima	N. × mixta (fournieri)	northiana × maxima
N. × boisiana	tiveyi × hookeriana	N. × mizuho	rafflesiana × dyeriana
N. × boissiense	gracilis × superba	N. × morganiana	mirabilis × hookeriana
N. × caroli-schmidtii	mixta × tiveyi	N. × nagoya	mixta × thorelii
N. × chelsonii	dominii × hookeriana	N. × nakanogo	mirabilis × rafflesiana
N. × chelsonii excellens	rafflesiana × dominii × hookeriana	N. × nasu	thorelii × wrigleyana
N. × coccinea	hookeriana × mirabilis	N. × nel horner	chelsonii × dominii
N. × compacta	hookeriana × mirabilis	N. × neufvilliana	mixta × maxima
N. × courtii	gracilis × dominii	N. × nobilis	sanguinea × maxima superba
N. × cylindrica	distillatoria × veitchii	N. × oiso or oisoensis	mixta × maxima superba
N. × dainty koto	thorelii × merrilliana	N. × okuyama	oiso × mirabilis
N. × deslogesii	tiveyi × mixta	N. × outramiana	sedenii × hookeriana
N. × dicksoniana	rafflesiana × veitchii	N. × paradisae	mirabilis × hookeriana
N. × dominii	rafflesiana × gracilis	N. × paullii	tiveyi × mixta
N. × dormanniana	mirabilis × sedenii	N. × petersii	mixta × tiveyi
N. × dreamy koto	thorelii × veitchii	N. × picturata	mixta × dicksoniana
N. × dyeriana	mixta × dicksoniana	N. × pitcheri	paradisae × henryana
N. × easeful koto	mirabilis × fukakusana	N. × princeps	mixta × dyeriana
N. × ecstatic koto	thorelii × maxima	N. × prosperity	lecouflei × dyeriana
N. × edinensis	rafflesiana × chelsonii	N. × ratcliffiana	mirabilis × hookeriana
N. × effulgent koto	mirabilis × thorelii	N. × rafflesiana pallida	dominii × rafflesiana
N. × emmarene	ventricosa × khasiana	N. × remilliensis	mixta × tiveyi
N. × excellens	rokko × mixta superba	N. × reutheri	mixta × mastersiana
N. × excelsa	veitchii × sanguinea	N. × robusta	mirabilis × hookeriana
N. × excelsior	rafflesiana × hookeriana	N. × roedigeri	mixta × maxima
N. × eyermanni	mirabilis × hookeriana	N. × rokko	thorelii × maxima
N. × facile koto	mastersiana × thorelii	N. × rubro-maculata	sedinii × veitchii
N. × festive koto	thorelii × balmy koto	N. × rufescens	distillatoria × intermedia
N. × formosa	chelsonii × distillatoria	N. × rutzii	mixta × tiveyi
N. × fukakusana	rafflesiana × dyeriana	N. × saint louis	chelsonii × dominii
N. × fulget koto	thorelii × fusca	N. × sedenii	gracilis × khasiana
N. × fushimiensis	globamphora × thorelii	N. × shaw (henry)	chelsonii × dominii
N. × fuso	oiso × khasiana	N. × shioji	mixta × dyeriana
N. × f.w. moore	mixta × dicksoniana	N. × siebertii	mixta × tiveyi
N. × gameri	tiveyi × mixta	N. × siebrechtiana	mirabilis × hybrida
N. × gautieri	= mixta (northiana × maxima)	N. × simonii	northiana × maxima
N. × goebelii	mixta × maxima	N. × splendiana	kampotiana × mixta
N. × goettingensis	mixta × dicksoniana	N. × sprendida	mirabilis × hookeriana
N. × grandis	maxima superba × northiana	N. × stammieri	mixta × maxima
N. × hachijo	lecouflei × mirabilis	N. × stewartii	mirabilis × hookeriana
N. × hamakumiko	oiso × sohma	N. × superba	hookeriana × sedenii
N. × harryana (p. 122)	edwardsiana × villosa	N. × suzue kondo	mixta × thorelii
N. × henryana	sedenii × hookeriana	N. × takayuki sakai	tobaica × thorelii
N. × henry shaw	chelsonii × dominii	N. × tiveyi	maxima superba × veitchii
N. × hibberdii	hookeriana × sedenii	N. × tokuyoshi kondo	saint louis × rafflesiana
N. × hoelscheri	mixta × rufescens	N. × toyoshimae	truncata × thorelii
N. × hookerae	rafflesiana × mirabilis	N. × tsujimoto	mastersiana × wrigleyana
N. × hybrida	khasiana × gracilis	N. × vallierae	tiveyi × mixta
N. × île de france	lecouflei × mixta	N. × ville de rouen (p. 42)	mastersiana × wrigleyana
N. × intermedia	gracilis × rafflesiana	N. × williamsii	sedenii × hookeriana
N. × issey	alata × burkei	N. × wittei	maxima × stenophylla
N. × junghuhnii	sanguinea × singalana	N. × wrigleyana	mirabilis × hookeriana
N. × katherine moore	chelsonii × dominii	N. × yatomi	thorelii × veitchii
N. × khasiata	khasiana × ventrata	N. × yoyogi	ventricosa × deaniana

Note *on the hybrids of* Nepenthes:

Nepenthes hybrids from the same parents can be very different from each other. Even in the same sowing, some plants are green whilst others have a red pigmentation. The ascidia are also very different from one plant to the next and they are even more diversified if the plants belong to opposite sexes. This explains the different names which have been attributed to the same hybrid. The name to use, or 'grex', is the oldest one and it must be followed by the name of the variety or cultivar. The list given here allows the recognition of labelled plants which one finds in various botanical gardens or those owned by enthusiasts.

Glossary

Acuminate Narrowing suddenly to a point.

Acute Narrowing gradually to a point.

Alternate Arranged singly along an axis, at different levels. *Alternate organs, leaves.*

Amplexicaul Said of a leaf whose base clasps the branch and which, in *Nepenthes*, narrows gradually.

Anther End of the stamen, bearing the pollen.

Apex End part or top.

Ascidium Leaf transformed into a trumpet. Synonym: urn.

Asexual Of no sex. *Asexual reproduction*: reproduction by non-sexual means.

Attenuated Diminishing in width or thickness.

Axillary Growing from the base of a leaf. *Axillary organ.*

Bilabial Having two lips, through an incomplete joining of the sepals or petals. *Bibabial corolla, calyx.*

Bracted Leaf atrophied on the flower stalks or a modified leaf between the flower and the leaf.

Bulb Swollen or rounded underground part, composed of a layer of fleshy scales and a bud.

Calyx External surround of the flower formed by the sepals.

Canaliculate Grooved like a gutter.

Carnivorous SEE Insectivorous.

Ciliate With hairs protruding from the margin.

Cordate Heart-shaped.

Corolla All the petals of a flower.

Corymb An inflorescence whose flower stalks are longer on the outside so that all the flowers are at about the same level.

Cultivar Plant variety obtained in cultivation.

Cuneiform Wedge-shaped or angled.

Decumbent Lying along the ground.

Dichotomous Dividing into two.

Dioecious Having male and female flowers on separate plants.

Dolomite Rock containing calcium often used in the cultivation medium of certain plants.

Ellipsoid Solid with an obtuse extremity whose longitudinal axis is one and a half or twice as long as the transverse axis.

Endemic A plant native to a specific region that is not found elsewhere in natural conditions.

Enzyme Organic substance that acts as a catalyst in biochemical reactions and helps digestion.

Epiphyte Plant living on another (usually a tree) without being a parasite of it.

Fimbriate With a finely cut edge, like a fringe.

Fungicide Product used for the treatment of fungal diseases.

Gemma Sort of small bud, produced by the plant and able to form a new plant identical to the mother plant.

Glabrous Having no hair.

Hermaphrodite Said of a plant having organs of both sexes.

Heterophyll Said of a plant having dissimilar leaves.

Hibernaculum Bud of certain plants formed in order to withstand the rigours of winter and to renew the plant in spring.

Homophyll Said of a plant whose leaves are all the same.

Inflorescence Floral part of the plant.

Infundibular Funnel-shaped.

Insectivorous Capturing insects and absorbing the nutritional matter from them. *Insectivorous plant.*

Intergeneric A hybrid resulting from a cross between two different genera.

Lanceolate Shaped like a lance, narrowing to a point.

Limb Main part of the leaf after the petiole.

Linear Long and narrow, with edges more or less parallel.

Oblong Longer than wide and rounded at both ends.

Obovate Egg-shaped, but with the narrow end below the middle; inversely ovate.

Obtuse With a rounded top.

Operculum Lid, covering the urn partially or completely, closed when young, then open, but unable to move.

Orbicular More or less circular.

Ovary Part of the pistil containing the seeds.

Ovoid Egg-shaped.

Pedicel A small stem bearing a flower or an organ.

Peduncle The stalk of an inflorescence.

Peltate More or less circular and flat with the stalk inserted underneath in the middle.

Penniform Set on either side of an axis, like the barbs of a feather.

Perianth All the sepals and petals, making up the calyx and the corolla respectively.

Peristome Sort of crown situated at the top of the ascidia of *Nepenthes*, curved downwards on either side and made of rings extending on the inside into sharp teeth.

Perlite Natural silicate in particle form.

Petiole Lower part of the leaf, which joins the limb to the branch.

pH Indicator of the concentration of hydrogen ions in a solution. Above pH 7, the solution is alkaline; below this it is acid.

Pistil Female flower organ, comprising the ovary, the style, and the stigma.

Polypody A species of fern, genus *Polypodium*, often growing on moist rocks or walls. The roots of this plant, without the rhizomes, are used in certain composts.

Prostrate Lying on the ground.

Pubescent Covered with fine, short hair.

Radical Growing directly from the root. *Radical leaf.*

Reniform Kidney-shaped.

Rhizome Underground branch or one just showing on the surface, giving rise to roots and branches.

Rosette Collection of radical leaves forming a circle.

Sessile Leaf, flower or organ fixed directly to the branch, with no stalk.

Spathulate Spoon-shaped, wide at the top, narrowing towards the base.

Sphagnum Lime-hating moss from damp sites.

Spur Appendage of variable shape on a trumpet.

Stalk Thin stem bearing the flowers.

Stamen Organ containing or bearing pollen.

Stigma Upper part of the pistil, which receives the pollen grains during fertilization.

Stolon Slender branch at the base of a plant, which lengthens and gives rise to leaves able to form new individuals.

Style Elongated part above the ovary carrying the stigmas at its apex.

Tomentose Covered in dense, interwoven hairs, like down.

Trigonal Having three angles.

Tuber Underground swelling of the branch containing a food store and having an eye or several buds.

Ubiquitous Having a wide geographical spread around the world; seen everywhere.

Urceolate Urn-shaped or in the shape of a round bell with a narrow mouth.

Utricle Organ in the shape of a wineskin capable of capturing prey.

Variety Plant that differs from others of its species in one or more characteristics of shape or colour. Abbreviation 'var.'.

Vermiculite Mineral substance formed from the deterioration of mica and biotite and used as part of the cultivation mediums of some plants.

Tendril Filament of varying dimensions special to climbing plants and having the ability to wind round a support.

Bibliography

A list of plates, up to 1938, of each genus and species can be found in the *Index Londiniensis*, in eight volumes (the Royal Horticultural Society, London).

Baffray (M.), Brice (Fr.) et Danton (Ph.), *Les Plantes carnivores de France*, Séquences, 134 p., 1985.

Cheers (Gordon), *Carnivorous Plants*, Globe Press, Melbourne, 95 p., 1983 (C).

Danser (B.H.), 'The Nepenthaceae of the Netherland Indies', *Bulletin du jardin botanique de Buitenzorg*, 200 p., 1928.

Darwin (Charles), *Insectivorous Plants*, 1875.

Erickson (Rica), *Plants of Prey in Australia*, Lamb Publications, Osborne Park, Western Australia, 94 p., 1968 (C).

Fessler (Alfred), *Fleischfressende Pflanzen*, Kosmos, Stuttgart, 112 p., 1982 (C).

Graf (A.B.), *Encyclopédie Exotica*, Roehrs Company, several editions since 1957.

Graf (A.B.), *Encyclopédie Tropica*, Roehrs Company, several editions since 1978 (C).

Jolivet (Pierre), *Les Plantes carnivores*, Le Rocher, Monaco, 126 p., 1987.

Kondo (K. & M.), *Carnivorous Plants of the World*, Ienohikari Association, Tokyo, Japanese text, 230 p., 1983 (C).

Kurata (Shigeo), *Nepenthes of Mount Kinabulu*, Sabah National Parks Trustees, Sabah, Malaysia, 80 p., 1976 (C).

Lloyd (F.E.), *The Carnivorous Plants*, Ronald Press, New York, 352 p., 1942.

Lowrie (Allan), *Carnivorous Plants of Australia*, vol 1. (three other volumes in preparation), University of Western Australia Press, 200 p., 1987 (C).

Macfarlane, *Das Pflanzenreich, Droseraceae*, Wilhelm Englemann, Leipzig and Berlin, 1906.

Macfarlane, *Das Pflanzenreich, Sarraceniaceae, Nepenthaceae*, Wilhelm Englemann, Leipzig and Berlin, 1908.

Overbeck (Cynthia), *Carnivorous Plants*, Lerner, Minneapolis, 48 p., 1982 (C).

Pietropaolo (James & Patricia), *The World of Carnivorous Plants*, R.J. Stoneridge, Shortsville, New York, 128 p., 1974.

Pietropaola (James & Patricia), *Carnivorous Plants of the World*, Timber Press, Portland, USA, 206 p., 1986 (C).

Poole (Lynne & Gray), *Insect-eating Plants*, Crowell, New York, 87 p., 1963.

Schnell (D.E.), *Carnivorous Plants of the U.S.A and Canada*, Blair, 125 p., 1976 (C).

Schwartz (Randall), *Carnivorous Plants*, Praeger Publishers, New York and Washington, 128 p., 1974.

Slack (Adrian), *Carnivorous Plants*, Ebury Press, 240 p., 1979 (C).

Slack (Adrian), *Insect-eating Plants*, Alpha Books, 172 p., 1986 (C).

(C) indicates that the work contains colour photographs.

Carnivorous plant societies

Of the principal societies that publish bulletins, these are the addresses of the best known:

France: Centre de Documentation sur le Milieu Naturel (C.D.M.), 55, rue Louis-Ricard, 76000 Rouen.
Germany: Gesellschaft für fleischfressende Pflanzen im deutschsprachigen Raum, c/o Rolf-Diether Golthardt, Adenauerstrasse 13, D-7303 Neuhausen.
Australia: Australian Carnivorous Plant Society, P.O. Box 256, Goodwood, South Australia 5034; Brisbane Carnivorous Plant Society, Eugenia Street, Inala, Queensland 4077; Victorian Carnivorous Plants Society, c/o Stefanie Hamel, 1, Osborne Grove, Preston, Victoria 3072; Ipswich Carnivorous Plant Society, 57, Edward Street, Flinders View, Queensland 4305.

USA: The International Carnivorous Plant Society, Fullerton Arboretum, Department of Biology, California State University, Fullerton CA 92634.
Great Britain: The Carnivorous Plant Society, 174 Baldwins Lane, Croxley Green, Herts WD3 3LQ.
Japan: Insectivorous Plant Society of Japan, Department of Biology, Nippon Dental College, 9-20-1 Chome, Fujimi, Chiyoda-ku, Tokyo.
New Zealand: New Zealand Carnivorous Plant Society, P.O. Box 162, Christchurch.